Dr. D. James Kennedy was my friend for over 20 years. I admired him for many reasons—foremost was his extreme trust in God, the Bible, and his passion to share the Gospel with everyone who would listen. Evangelism Explosion is just one of the many ministries Dr. Kennedy founded. By reading *Well Done*, you will see that the same great passion that burned within Jim Kennedy is still alive and thriving today within the leadership of his and my long term friend, John Sorensen.

—BOBB BIEHL
Executive Mentor, BobbBiehl.com

Dr. D. James Kennedy was well known for his passion for the Gospel of Jesus Christ. Now, Dr. John B. Sorensen has written a book that combines that same passion with a thoughtful examination of what it truly means to be a servant of Jesus. *Well Done* will challenge readers and help strengthen their faith.

—JAMES D. DALY
President, Focus on the Family

I cannot think of a more timely book for the Body of Christ than *Well Done* by D. James Kennedy and John Sorensen. This visionary masterpiece moves us from the short look to the long look and from being so wrapped up with what others around think about us to what God above thinks about our life. Every Christian who reads *Well Done* will gain an eternal glimpse of what truly pleases the Lord both now and forever!

—DR. JAMES O. DAVIS
Cofounder, Billion Soul Network

D. James Kennedy founded, developed and led by example the ministry of Evangelism Explosion for over 40 years. In this book John Sorensen demonstrates very convincingly that Dr. Kennedy's passion and vision for EE is in competent and trustworthy hands under his leadership. "Well Done" is well done and will encourage and energize your heart in new ways for fulfilling the great commission.

—DR. STERLING HUSTON
Chair, EE International Board

The names of two men appear on the cover of this book. It has been my privilege to know both. They both shared—I write in that tense because D. James Kennedy has gone to be with his Lord—a deep and active commitment to making the Gospel of Jesus Christ known in all the world. As the Founder and first President of Evangelism Explosion, Jim Kennedy created a movement for training and multiplying disciples and disciple-makers that has spread around the world. As the current President of EE, John Sorensen brings a passion for, and a commitment to, winning people to Christ and for training them to win others which is fired by his love for Christ, his desire to hear the words "Well done.", and his love and admiration for Jim Kennedy.

This book will challenge and disturb but in the best possible way. Its intention is to stimulate all of us to be about our Lord's business in the world. My hope is that many will read *Well Done* and be inspired to seek that commendation on their own lives and service.

—THE MOST REVEREND R. H. GOODHEW
ArchBishop of the Anglican Church, Retired
AO, Th.L, MCD, MA, D.Litt.

Well Done challenges its readers to consider what it truly means to live a life worthy of the calling they have received. Evangelism Explosion has been a pioneer in global evangelism and continues to be a critical tool for the proclamation of the good news in the world today. Kennedy and Sorensen display with rich and engaging clarity what it looks like to be a disciple of Christ and how we are to be "big picture" visionaries, sold out for Christ and His mission. I have personally experienced Sorensen's visionary leadership through the initiation of a OneHope/Kid's EE partnership that will reach upwards of 20 million children worldwide. That is a monumental task, by God's grace, culminating in a heavenly declaration: "Well Done".

—ROB HOSKINS
President, OneHope

In our fifty plus years of married life, Jim was ready always to share with others the eternal hope that he possessed. His life was consistent with what he preached and was a shining example and encouragement to me. I'm thankful that John is faithful and is carrying on what began many years ago.

—ANNE KENNEDY

The most important day for the believer and non-believer alike is when, at the end of our lives, we stand before Jesus Christ. Here is an important new book by the late Dr. D. James Kennedy and Dr. John Sorensen, his hand-picked successor in the worldwide ministry of Evangelism Explosion. This book is geared toward preparing us for that all important day, that we may live in such a way as to hear those words out of the mouth of Jesus, "Well done, thou good and faithful servant."

—DR. JERRY NEWCOMBE
Host of Dr. Kennedy's *The Coral Ridge Hour* and author/co-author of 21 books

As a lifelong Southern Baptist, I've been inspired by Dr. Kennedy. His knowledge, vision, and example combined to direct everyone's attention toward His Lord. Having attended denominational schools all my life, I was frankly shocked to find a Presbyterian who was more passionate about the Great Commission than anyone I'd ever met. Joining a mighty army around the globe, I took heart from this giant of the faith.

This book, however, is more than a tribute to DJK; it provides an answer to one of the hotly debated election questions of our day—where do works fit into the equation? More than that, it explores the passing of the baton from the founder of EE to the current President, John Sorensen. Such a baton is often dropped with much loss to the Kingdom. In this study, you'll find that EE is continuing to multiply around the world.

As Dr. Kennedy often said "Discouragement is Satan's greatest weapon against evangelism". I hardily recommend *Well Done* to Christians of every nation, language and people group as an exhortation against weariness in doing well.

—DR. DAVID SELF
Executive Pastor, Houston's First Baptist Church

I consider both D. James Kennedy and John Sorensen a friend of mine and recommend that you read the book *Well Done* to get a new perspective on the work for which God has called you to do. I first met D. James Kennedy when he was working towards a doctors degree at Winona Lake Summer School of Theology, Indiana. He was a diligent worker and went on to finish that degree at New York University. Then I met John Sorensen in the last ten years and God has used him to lead Evangelism Explosion to new heights in the work of

God. May God motivate you in His work as you read and contemplate this thoughtful insight.

—DR. ELMER L. TOWNS
Co-Founder, Liberty University
Dean, School of Religion

Excellence in all things and all things to God's glory! That was the life and ministry standard of Dr. D. James Kennedy, and it was contagious! Dr. John Sorensen saw that standard lived out in Dr. Kennedy's life, embracing it as his own. These many years later, Dr. Sorensen and Dr. Kennedy have written a marvelous book that details and exemplifies a life that is intentional, purposeful, and well-lived. *Well Done* is far more than an exhortation; it is a biblical roadmap to living out your high and holy calling.

—FRANK WRIGHT, PH.D.
President & CEO, National Religious Broadcasters

WELL DONE

A Christian Doctrine of Works

D. James Kennedy, Ph.D
John B. Sorensen, D.D.

GreenTree Press
Fort Lauderdale

Edited by Jerry Newcomb and Hannah Sorensen.

Published in Fort Lauderdale, Florida by GreenTree Press.

Library of Congress Control Number: 2010910810

ISBN: 978-0-9828721-0-9

Printed in the United States of America

Even though the book is written in my voice, half the content you will read comes from the late Dr. D. James Kennedy, a man after God's own heart. Anything positive that you take from this book probably came from him, and any mistakes that you see—those are probably mine. So for my first "to" as an author:

To Dr. D James Kennedy—beloved Pastor, Mentor, Founder, and Friend. God used you in mighty ways to touch many lives, and the fruit of your labors was more like an orchard for God. Soli Deo Gloria.

Table of Contents

FINISH

Foreword

By Mr. Rich Devos

Well Done. Now those are two words we all want to hear. Whether in this life or eternity with Christ, we want to be told, "I'm proud of you! You did it! Well done!" It is not much different from when my grandchildren try to get my attention and acknowledgement. They could be riding a bike or sliding into a pool, but they always cry out, "Watch me! Watch me, Grandpa!" They want to know that I am watching them; so in turn, I can tell them how proud I am of what they have done.

Dear reader, God is watching you. He is watching your actions, waiting for the day He can tell you, His precious child, "Well done. I'm so proud of you." He wants you to live a life full of love and full of Him. He is watching for you to complete the work which He has given you—work which will bring Him glory and pleasure. And guess what? You can do it!

When Amway opened in Russia, I called over there to speak to six hundred people coming into Amway. My entire message was on, "You can do it!" and they were so excited that they were singing, dancing, and cheering—it was more like a football game than business meeting.

Those Russian people were excited by the idea of being free to have their own businesses and doing something of substance. The theme of "You can do it" was incredibly powerful to them. So how much more so should it be powerful to us? God gave His only begotten Son for you and me to be free from sin. We have freedom in Him!

He has also given us every gift and resource that we need to complete the work in which He has given us. He has given us something of incredible substance to do on this earth! We should be thoroughly excited by the fact that we can do the work He has given us because our Heavenly, loving Father wants nothing more than to see us succeed. He wants to wish us, "Well done, my good and faithful servant." You can do the work which He has given you. For the glory of Christ, you can live a "Well Done" life!

This book was written for the very purpose of you being able to see that you can do it. It outlines what God has given you to do, how you can be a faithful servant to God, and what a "Well Done" life looks like. I pray you can take hope from these coming pages to do the work He has given you on this earth before you reach your hope everlasting.

And always remember, dear reader, God is looking down on you wanting you to succeed; so on that day that you finally see Him face to face, He can say, "I'm so proud of you. Well done." Never lose sight of that.

Love ya!

Rich

Parable of the Talents

*F*or the kingdom of heaven is like a man traveling to a far country, who called his own servants and delivered his goods to them. And to one he gave five talents, to another two, and to another one, to each according to his own ability; and immediately he went on a journey. Then he who had received the five talents went and traded with them, and made another five talents. And likewise he who had received two gained two more also. But he who had received one went and dug in the ground, and hid his lord's money. After a long time the lord of those servants came and settled accounts with them.

So he who had received five talents came and brought five other talents saying, 'Lord, you delivered to me five talents; look, I have gained five more talents besides them.' His lord said to him, 'Well done, good and faithful servant; you were faithful over a few things, I will make you ruler over many things. Enter into the joy of your lord.' He also who had received two talents came and said, 'Lord, you delivered to me two talents; look, I have gained two more talents besides them.' His lord said to him, 'Well done, good and faithful servant; you have been faithful over a few *things, I will make you ruler over many things. Enter into the joy of your lord.'*

Then he who had received the one talent came and said, 'Lord, I knew you to be a hard man, reaping where you have not sown, and gathering where you have not scattered seed. And I was afraid, and went and hid your talent in the ground. Look, there you have what is yours.'

But his lord answered and said to him, 'You wicked and lazy servant, you knew that I reap where I have not sown, and gather where I have not scattered seed. So you ought to have deposited my money with the bankers, and at my coming I would have received back my own with interest. So take the talent from him, and give it to him who has ten talents.

'For everyone who has, more will be given, and he will have abundance; but from him who does not have, even what he has will be taken away. And cast the unprofitable servant into the outer darkness. There will be weeping and gnashing of teeth' (Matthew 25:14-30).

Introduction

One night, I was watching an interview of Dr. Billy Graham on television. I do not know why the interviewer had the presence to ask this question of him, but she gently quizzed, "Dr. Graham, when you get to Heaven one day, what do you most hope to hear from God?"

He steadily replied, "Well done." We all probably would have answered in the same way.

Then she proceeded to ask him another very perceptive question, "Do you expect to hear it?"

He cast his eyes toward the ground. A few seconds went by before he lifted his eyes back to hers and replied, "I honestly am not sure if I've done enough to hear 'Well done' from God."

This was from Billy Graham! "If Billy Graham has not done enough to hear 'Well done' from God," I thought, "we are in a lot of trouble!"

So I began to ponder, "Well, what is it that would lead someone to say that?" I started asking congregations all over the world, "How many of you all want to hear the words, 'Well done' when you get to Heaven?"

Almost every hand goes up. Actually, I am always curious about the ones who do not raise their hands. I follow then with a second question, "How many of you all expect to hear it?"

In this little, informal survey that I conducted, almost every hand went up every time.

I used to think, "What is it that these people know that Billy Graham doesn't know?" But now I think the question is actually more fairly asked the other way around. What is it that Billy Graham knows that these congregations do not?

When I brought up Dr. Graham's interview to Dr. Kennedy one day, a conversation started between us that went on for over a year as we thought about and talked about what it would mean to hear "Well done" from God. We poured over the statistics that I was bringing back from the congregations I spoke at. I asked him, "Why do you think this is? Why is there such a big difference between Billy Graham and the rest of the church of Jesus Christ?" As we began to talk, we discovered that there were only three reasons we could come up with.

The first reason is that the people who were hearing the questions were not listening. They were half asleep; and when they saw everyone else's hands go up, they thought, "Well, I better put my hand up too!" Or perhaps there was some sort of peer pressure that caused them to think, "That ought to be the right answer!" so they stuck their hand up.

They did not really believe it, but they raised their hand because they thought they were supposed to.

Another possibility would be congregations suddenly (at least in this area) became "calvinistic."[1] They thought, "What Jesus did on the cross gets applied to me. And when He says 'Well done', He's not really saying 'Well done' to me; he's saying 'Well done' because of what Christ did on the cross. "However, to defend that theory, you would not be able to use the Bible. You might be able to use other books, but the Bible will not help you. The Word of God contains Matthew 25:14-30, The Parable of the Talents, which clearly describes the reason why some will hear "Well done" and others will not.

Now there is a third reason we came up with and this is perhaps the most disturbing of all. I believe this reason to be the most accurate reason for why most people in the Christian church today will raise their hand and say that they expect to hear *"Well done, my good and faithful servant."* It is because people genuinely believe that God does not care about what they do with their time, about what they do with their money, about what they do with their talents, and about what they do with the resources that have been given to them. They really think that when they

---

[1] Calvinism is the Protestant theological system of John Calvin and his successors, which develops Luther's work on the justification by faith alone in Christ alone (drawing from the work of many Church fathers—like Augustine and the Apostle Paul), and emphasizes the grace of God in salvation by the substitutionary atonement of Christ's work on the cross. While this is quite correct as the means of salvation, it is not a correct way to view man's responsibility in the works God has assigned for him to do.

came in the door to become a Christian that all that had to happen was for them to accept Jesus to get to Heaven, and that everything between that moment and the moment that they see Jesus face to face is for naught. Doesn't matter. God doesn't care. I can spend my money on whatever I want to. I can do whatever I want to with my time. I can do whatever I want to with my talents. It simply does not matter to God.

That is the only answer that makes sense to me. And that is the way we live regardless of what we say.

But, dear friend, be not discouraged. For both the new and the veteran Christian who asks, "How can I hear, 'Well done' from God? Can I make God smile? Is there really a Christian Doctrine of Works?", we wrote this book for you to help you do the things that God has commanded of you to be that faithful servant.

Just to be extremely clear, this does not mean that we work for our salvation. That is, by the way, the most universally held religious belief on the planet Earth. Do good, and you get to Heaven. Some people may read this and immediately go to that. Please, if you do think like this, you have missed it—not just by a little. You have missed it by one hundred and eighty degrees. You cannot save yourself through good works; it cannot be done by anybody.

Then what are we talking about? In Ephesians 2:10, it says, *"For we are His workmanship, created in Christ*

Jesus for good works, which God prepared beforehand that we should walk in them." What we are talking about, the Christian Doctrine of "Do", is about what I would need to "do" to hear, "Well done." We do good works out of gratitude for what Jesus has done and the desire to be His faithful servants unto the end of our lives, when our "doing" becomes "done." There were two servants in this parable who understood this concept. They did not have any problem with it, and they immediately went to work to turn what God gave them into something more. And when their work was done and the Master came back, they were praised for it.

My prayer is that through studying the Christian doctrine of "do" together, you and I can learn what it is to be faithful workers of God and "doers" for His kingdom. Then maybe one day, you and I will hear from the lips of our Savior, Jesus Christ, "Well done. You did what it was that I asked you to do. I put you in charge of a few things, and you did it! Now I am going to put you in charge of more."

Jim Kennedy is now in Heaven with our Savior who I believe greeted him whole heartedly as a loving Shepherd to His prized sheep, as a Master to His favorite servant, as a Father to His most beloved child with the words, "Well done, My good and faithful servant." He, as my co-writer for this book, would have wished for the same thing for us: that we would learn to apply our resources, time, money, and talents for God's glory. Make that investment so when the Master returns for us someday, we can give Him all that is His for the glory of God. Then we will hear those ever-longed for words from our Master, *"Well Done."*

May it be. Amen.

Do

Part I

1

The Big Picture

(The Christian Doctrine of "Do")

"Go therefore and make disciples of all the nations, baptizing them in the name of the Father and of the Son and of the Holy Spirit."

Matthew 28:19

It seems to me that there are two types of Christians in this world. Now, this may not be very scientific, but I am going to liken them to animals—albeit strange ones.

The first type are buffalo Christians. Buffalos have big necks, and they cannot move their heads around much. Because of this, they end up spending their lives looking down at the ground. All they see is their feet, where they are about to walk, and what it is that they are about to eat. That's it. Talk about no vision. But what would they need vision for? They are buffalo. All they need to see is that small patch of ground.

In the other group, you have the giraffe Christians. They are not stuck looking at the grass. With their long necks, they can see the expanse of the savanna. That is the issue here. The vision. It is important to be able to see the proper perspective, and the passage in Matthew 25:14-30 tells us this: our attitude matters. Do not be a grumbler. Be wary of becoming a buffalo Christian who situates himself/ herself on a little bit of territory, complaining against God and coming up with nonsense that God does not love you and that He is not "just" in what He does. That is what happens with the servant in the Parable of the Talents who hears, "Get out!" and not "Well done." The ones who hear "Well done" are the servants who are willing to look to God and say, "This is Yours, and we are Your servants. Everything we have is Yours." These servants are giraffe Christians. They are Big Picture people.

We so often forget about perspective and forget to be like the Godly servants. Proper perspective leads to a proper attitude, which leads to action. You may ask, "How? How do we gather a proper perspective on where we are with Jesus as Lord of our lives? How do we serve Him with the actions and activities of our lives and be completely sold out to Him? Where do we get guidance on these topics?" I would submit to you that we get it from the very Word of God.

PERSPECTIVE

Sammy grew up in Beirut, Lebanon. As he saw the hollow reality of the religious fervor around him, he made the determination to live for no one but himself. He would work hard, make a lot of money, and live life his way.

Soon he was through school and working as a waiter at an international hotel. He was living his plan, and then he met an elderly couple. This couple made friends with Sammy as they ate in his section every week. They had been trained in Evangelism Explosion and were always looking for opportunities that God might give them to share. After one year, Sammy finally listened to the Gospel and gave his heart to Christ.

Now that he was a Christian, he thought he should do what Christians do. The only example he had was that of the elderly couple who had gone out of their way to care for Sammy. So his life plan changed. Now he would live life for others, and he began to do just that.

Some time later, while working at a hotel in Jerusalem, Sammy came across another young man, 22 years of age, in the hotel lounge. Sammy befriended this young man, shared the Gospel with him, and helped him to see what his life could be with Christ. That young man committed his life to Christ. You have heard of him. His name is Franklin Graham. Though Franklin grew up in a Christian home and was the son of America's best-known evangelist (Billy Graham), he was a prodigal son for years, until God used Sammy to turn him around.

What started as an elderly couple simply determining to live for others has led to many thousands, perhaps millions, who have been blessed by what God has done through Franklin and Sammy. Sammy today is a pastor in Beirut. A while ago I received a report that Sammy's church members fed over 30,000 people displaced from their homes by war in that region.

What a change in perspective.

Every one of us faces this challenge to live our lives our way or to live our lives God's way, and God made it very clear how He would have us live: for others.

John Maxwell said, "The entire population of the world —with one minor exception—is composed of others."[2]

Albert Einstein said, "A person first starts to live when he can live outside himself."[3]

I wish I could say that we are all there. I mean I know it sounds like common sense, yet not everyone gets the Big Picture or practices selfless living. Instead, many grownups live like perpetual toddlers. They live by the toddler's code, which goes something like this:

If I like it, it is mine.

If I can take it away from you, it is mine.

---

[2] John Maxwell and I were talking about this very topic. We served together on a steering committee that was formed out of a global vision to see, God-willing, five million new churches planted and one billion people come to Christ in the next fifteen years. This steering committee has become known as the Billion Soul Network (www.Billion.tv), consisting of more than one thousand denominations and organizations in every world region. John discusses this principle at length in his book *Winning With People*.

[3] Kevin Harris, "Collected Quotes from Albert Einstein" 1995. You can find this quote at: http://rescomp.stanford.edu/~cheshire/EinsteinQuotes.html.

If I had it a while ago, it is mine.

If I say it is mine, it is mine.

If it looks like mine, it is mine.

If I saw it first, it is mine.

If you're having fun with it, it is definitely mine.

If you lay it down, it is mine.

If it is broken, it is yours.[4]

What a perspective. And how wrong it is. It is interesting to note that an egotist is not someone who thinks too much of himself. It is someone who thinks too little of others. In some ways, the opposite of loving others is not hating others, but self-centeredness.

The shame of it is that ultimately the things that bring us the greatest joy involve others; and we, many times, miss it.

WHOSE LIFE IS IT ANYWAY?

There is a beautiful picture of a Godly man who pressed on toward maturity and completely washed away from all forms of toddler-hood. Do you remember the day when God was about to take Elijah up to Heaven (2 Kings 2:1-14)? Elijah said to Elisha, *"Stay here at Gilgal."* Gilgal was the place where the Israelites entered the Promised

---

[4] Author unknown.

Land for the first time. It was also where Elisha was from. In a way, Gilgal represents a place of "firsts." I think there was a sense in which Elijah was saying, "Stay here at the starting line" as a challenge to see what Elisha would do. Elisha said, "No way. I'm going where you're going."

How many times do folks get saved, come in the door, sit down to rest, and fall asleep? They end up staying at Gilgal, the place where they started.

I have spoken with many believers who have gotten trapped in this first "me" stage of Christianity. "Me, me, me. It's all about me. Forget about you. Let's talk about me!" For them, worship is about them. They want their preferences met. They rate their pastor by what he does for them. They insist on their worship style. It is an awful trap that we must avoid.

Next Elijah said, *"Stay here at Bethel."* But Elisha refused. Bethel was the place where God spoke to Jacob. Jacob named it Bethel, or house of God, because God had spoken to him there. In a way, Bethel was a place of learning and worship. There were prophets there who could tell people what God had said.

There are many Christians who are satisfied to come to Christ and then get involved in worship and learning. They spend their whole lives sitting at the feet of the teachers soaking it up. But to what end? It seems to be merely their own personal edification. This is another trap that we must avoid.

Next Elijah and Elisha travel to Jericho, a place of a grand triumph for God's people. Elijah said, *"Stay here,"* but Elisha refuses.

Many fall into the trap of camping out at a place of past victory. Their whole lives become defined by one moment. Everything is seen in that light. "Those were the days!" is the mantra. If God has blessed our efforts at some point, it would be easy to sit down there and rest. But we must not.

Last Elijah and Elisha traveled over the Jordan River to that place that God would take Elijah up to Heaven. The Jordan many times symbolizes in Scripture the crossing over from one life to the next. And in a sense, this is what Elisha did. He crossed over a servant and came back a prophet. He gave up his life to the Lord's service and in turn got a new and better life.

What a joy it is to see Christians come to this final place of complete surrender to whatever the Lord has called them to. They have crossed over. They have given up their lives for the cause of Christ. They have the vision, the perspective, and have realized literally what Paul meant when he said, *"You are not your own...you've been bought with a price"* (1 Corinthians 6:19-20).

That kind of Christian, living for God's glory and using the talents entrusted to him or her for the spreading of the Kingdom, is the key to reaching the world for Jesus. Which one are you?

A RIGHT PERSPECTIVE

Thankfully, the Bible contains instructions for us to change our attitude and get the right perspective on life. Look at the familiar passage of Matthew 28:18-20. This is commonly referred to as the Great Commission:

> *And Jesus came and spoke to them, saying, 'All authority has been given to Me in heaven and on earth. Go therefore and make disciples of all the nations, baptizing them in the name of the Father and of the Son and of the Holy Spirit, teaching them to observe all things that I have commanded you; and lo, I am with you always, even to the end of the age.' Amen.*

First, correct perspective comes from Christ's authority (verse 18). Jesus is the one true authority for my life, and not only for me, but also for you, and the entire world.

Think about the statement, *"All authority in heaven and earth has been given to Me."* Could anyone else except Jesus truthfully say that? When Satan tested Jesus, he only offered Him the authority on earth. But God gave Jesus the authority of not only earth, but Heaven as well. All authority is His. He made everything, He holds all things together, and He is the only wise God, infinite in His knowledge and power.

For us to have the right perspective, we need to see Jesus in this light. Because He has the power, He gives us His command.

And that brings us to the second point: correct perspective comes from Christ's command (verse 19-20a).

In the Greek, the main verb in this passage is not "go". It is "make disciples." The go is assumed. "While you are going, make disciples" is the idea. Making disciples is our purpose.

There is a logical question here then. What is a disciple? Probably the best definition that I have ever heard is this: a disciple is a learning follower of Christ. With it comes the idea of progression and growth. You cannot stay where you are and be a learning follower of Christ. It is not like, "I got saved. I got my ticket to Heaven. I'm going to sit here and wait for Jesus to come back. And while I'm sitting here waiting, I guess I'll go about my business."

We must be about the process of growing in our knowledge of Christ and in our service to Him and His command. When we do not, we disappoint and disobey Him.

The writer to the Hebrews was writing to a group of people who should have been growing and progressing but were not. Hebrews 5:12-14 says this:

For though by this time you ought to be teachers, you need someone to teach you again the first principles of the oracles of God; and you have come to need milk and not solid food. For everyone who partakes only of milk is unskilled in the word of

9

righteousness, for he is a babe. But solid food belongs to those who are of full age."

There is a logical progression for a disciple-maker. Win people to Christ, build them in their faith, and send them out to do the same thing. That is what we do at Evangelism Explosion.

Dr. Kennedy called it spiritual multiplication. He dedicated his life to seeing it happen, as God made him able. In Evangelism Explosion, we live this out everyday. There are many people that God has allowed us to lead to Christ, teach them the foundations of the faith, and then get them involved in sharing their faith.

When people tell me that Evangelism Explosion does not work anymore, I laugh. How could they possibly be more wrong? It worked for me. I was led to the Lord through EE, trained in the foundations of the faith through Evangelism Explosion, taught to share that faith through EE, and then taught to teach others as well.

The point is, as Christians, we must be growing and helping others to grow as well. Southern Thailand is arguably one of the least evangelized spots on earth today. After the tsunami a few years back, the Lord opened doors that had never been open before in our lifetime. We had the opportunity to go in and cry with people there. We told them about Jesus and led over 60 of the Moken people group to Him.[5] Before the tsunami, they were an unreached people group. We worked with other groups to help six churches grow among this tribe and enlisted workers to go in and help them grow in Christ. Soon after, as God made us able, we trained them to share their new found faith with others in their tribe.

That is what we are talking about, and every one of us is to be part of it.

Win—Build—Send. This is the job of every Christian. In one form or another, we are all to work in God's vineyard. The jobs are varied, the laborers are different, but the goal is always the same: to build God's Kingdom on earth.

I do not know what you do for a living, but it is just a temporary job, so you can pay the bills. Your real job is making disciples with the unique set of gifts that God has given you.

A few years ago, I had the opportunity to lead devotions for the corporate staff of Chick-Fil-A in Atlanta, Georgia. Afterwards, I toured the offices. Dan Cathy, the son of the founder, Truit Cathy, came up to me and said, "You know, this is all just a front. We sell chicken, sure, but not to sell chicken. We sell chicken so that we can advance the Gospel of Jesus Christ around the world."

---

[5] The Moken are also known as "the Sea Gypsies" of southern Thailand. For more information, go to: http://www.joshuaproject.net/people-profile.php?rog3=TH&rop3=106723.

That is what each one of us should live for, and we should do it by growing as a disciple and making disciples. We need to have mentors in our lives, and we need to be mentors to others.

One of the best parts of being in Fort Lauderdale over the past fourteen years has been the time I have gotten to spend with Dr. Kennedy and Dr. Tom Stebbins. Both were and are committed to making disciples, and I have been privileged to be able to grow under them. One of the nicest compliments that I can receive is when people say, "I've really seen you grow over the past fourteen years." May God help me to grow until I die, and that I could help others to come to faith and grow as well.

We have a purpose as Christians. This is not an uncontrolled stroll through the byways of life. We are on a mission—a mission to follow Christ's command by making disciples.

Finally, correct perspective comes from Christ's promise. Jesus tells us in verse 20, *"Lo, I am with you always."*

One day I was chatting with an older man (Lance Bingham) in Australia; and he said, "I don't understand how you can fly so much. I could never get on so many planes crossing the ocean. I would be too afraid." I said, "You don't need to be afraid. Jesus has promised to be with you." He said, "Wait a minute now. That verse says LOW I am with you. I'm staying on the ground."

All humor aside, Jesus has promised us that He will always be with us. The book of Matthew begins with this. In Chapter 1:23 it reads, *"And they shall call His name Immanuel, which is translated 'God with us.'"* Now the book closes with the same reminder. Jesus says, "Immanuel, I AM (God) with you even unto the end of the age." What a promise. What a comfort. What a contrast with the other "world religions."

There are two thoughts about this promise. First, He helps you and me with all of our struggles. In fact, the Bible goes so far as to say that sometimes He carries us when we cannot go on. In Isaiah 46, God contrasts the gods of this world and Himself by saying (paraphrase), "Look at the gods of this world. Look how men swoop down and carry them and they are a great burden. Their backs hurt and their muscles strain at the weight." But we, on the other hand, do not carry God. He carries us. In Isaiah 46:4, God says, *"Even to your old age, I am He, and even to gray hairs I will carry you! I have made, and I will bear; even I will carry, and will deliver you."*

The second thought about this promise is this: because He is with me, He sees what I do. I find that thought to be very motivational. I do not know about you, but as a child I had a tendency to act a bit differently when my parents were around.

Jesus, the great authority of my life, is with me always. He sees me right now. He not only sees me, but He can see into my heart. He knows me. And what is most amazing to me is He loves me in spite of it all and wants to use me. This is truly amazing grace.

There are also other promises that Christ gives to bring us a proper perspective. In Matthew 28:20, He said, *"I am with you always, even to the end of the age."* In the Parable of the Talents, He is showing us a picture of the end of the age. The Master leaves on a long journey; and when he returns, he checks to see how his servants have done. What does that sound like to you? To me, it sounds very much like when Jesus ascended into Heaven and promised to return one day. And there are two points in this parable I am certain He is promising you.

First, Christ gives you talents—and do not think American Idol when you think talent—think resources, think your whole life, think all the things that He has made you able to do and be. He gave it to you according to your ability. Because He gave it to you according to your ability, the promise is that you are able to do the thing that Christ has called you to do. That is the first promise.

The second promise that is contained in Matthew 25:14-30 is this: He is going to inspect it one day. You will stand in front of a host of Heavenly people—but most importantly your Lord—and He is going to say, "How did you do?" That day is coming. And the purpose of this book is to help prepare you for that day.

The proper perspective for our life—for the world, for our actions, for our purpose, for our resources, for our energy, for our passion—comes when we get Christ's view and His perspective. Christ's authority, Christ's command, and Christ's promise. When we understand these points, our lives will be changed. What we do with our time will change. What we do with our money will change. We will be changed. Our focus will shift from ourselves to others— from ourselves to the world. We will want to do our Master's will and serve others. That, dear friend, is the Christian Doctrine of "Do."

There was a young man by the name of James Taylor. Not the singer who wrote "Fire and Rain," and "Shower the People You Love With Love." No, he was a different James Taylor. He was born in England in 1832 into a Christian family. His father was a pharmacist and a Methodist preacher. As he grew up, he became skeptical and worldly. He decided to live for this life only and left for school, eventually going into the banking business at the age of 15.

One day, when he was 17 years old, he went into his father's study and read a tract. One line specifically caught his attention. They were the words of Jesus when He said, "It is finished." He asked, "What is finished?" And not long after, when he knew the answer, he gave his heart to Christ, and his perspective on life completely changed. That young man no longer lived to get all that he could out of life. He no longer lived for himself. He began to live for Jesus and for others.

God called him into missions. He left his home and sailed for lands abroad. On March 1, 1854, at the age of 21 years, he reached Shanghai, China.

During his 51 years of service there, his China Inland Mission established 20 mission stations, brought 849 missionaries to the field, trained some 700 Chinese workers, raised four million dollars, and developed a witnessing Chinese church of 125,000. His gift for inspiring people to give themselves and their possessions to Christ was amazing. Some have called him the most widely used missionary in China's history.

James Taylor. James Hudson Taylor. A young boy that got the vision and became a Big Picture person. A man with the right perspective on what Jesus wanted him to be.

What a challenge that is to me. And, I hope, to you as well.

CONCLUSION

What we desperately need are men and women that will trust the Lord as deeply today as they plan to the day they die. We need Big Picture people.

J. Oswald Sanders said, "Eyes that look are common. Eyes that see are rare."[6] We need eyes that see the mission

---

[6] Vern McLellan, *Wise Words and Quotes* (Wheaton, IL: Tyndale House Publishers, 1998).

of Christ and hearts that yearn to follow. And I believe, more than anything else, we need eyes to see a proper perspective about what God wants us to do with the talents He gives us. Be a doer. Live for others. Serve your Master.

2

The Ten Commandments
For Today

(Do What He Says To Do)

*"And God spoke all these words, saying: 'I am the
Lord your God, who brought you out of the land of
Egypt, out of the house of bondage. You shall have
no other gods before Me."*

Exodus 20:1-3

The scorching desert, the dim presence, the
impenetrable cloud, the smoke as from a furnace, the
leaping flames, the trembling mountain, the voice of God
as the sound of thunder all conspired to cause the hearts of
Israel to tremble with fear and to melt within them. They
either fell upon their faces or they cried out saying to
Moses, *"You speak with us, and we will hear: but let not
God speak with us, lest we die"* (Exodus 20:19).

The Almighty came and sat, as it were, upon a gigantic
throne of granite to dispense His Law upon His creation.
These were the operating instructions from the Creator. Not

this time did God use the voice of a prophet, but spoke with His own voice. Not this time did He use the pen of a scribe, but God with His own finger reached out and wrote these things upon the tablet of stone Himself. He wrote the moral law—The Ten Commandments of God—for you and for me.

We begin our look at this Christian Doctrine of "Do" here in the beginning of the Bible by looking at the Ten Commandments, the moral law of God. We cannot understand the Good News of the Gospel until we understand the bad news of how we have broken God's law in every regard.

We will see later in this chapter how the Ten Commandments are for today—despite the fact some Christians deny that in our time. I heard about a young man who visited a church where the Ten Commandments were read aloud. He asked, "Why—since they are not for today?" Later on, coincidentally (or because of his lax view), his wife divorced him because of his recurrent infidelity.

BREAKING THE TEN COMMANDMENTS

It's important to note that it is impossible to break the Law of God. You cannot break the Law; you can only break yourself upon it. Innumerable individuals and nations have hurled themselves against those tablets of stone, and the remnants of their destruction may be found in the hospitals, the asylums, the prisons, the battlefields, and the skid rows of this world. You cannot break the Law of God; you can only break yourself upon it.

We live in a day and age where the Law of God is not thought kindly of in the public sphere. We seem to have dismissed it entirely. Judge Roy Moore, our 1997 Distinguished Christian Statesman Award Winner, had it on the wall in his courtroom and went through a great battle to keep it there.[7] Unfortunately, it was a battle that was lost. And now it is gone. No longer can you find the Law of God anywhere near the places where justice is dispensed in America. We have distanced ourselves from it. How did it happen? How did we get where we are today? Where did this disconnect begin?

Dr. Paul Johnson, one of the most eminent of modern historians has written a monumental work entitled *Modern Times* that catalogs and chronicles the twentieth century. In that, he points out that the twentieth century all began with the publication of a certain paper by a patent clerk. You may recall that in 1905, Albert Einstein released his special theory of relativity. In 1916 he published the general theory of relativity. In 1919, in the midst of an eclipse, it was ascertained that this theory was confirmed, and relativity became the watchword of the twentieth century.

---

[7] The D. James Kennedy Center for Christian Statesmanship was opened in 1995 to lift up the idea of Christian Statesmanship in the United States of America. Each year we present this award to a leader who exemplifies the ideal of Christian Statesmanship. To find out more go to: http://www.statesman.org.

Johnson points out that since that time, the entire twentieth century had been a spreading of the theory of relativity:

> ...out of the realm of physics and astronomy into every other science, and then into the social sciences of psychology and sociology, on into ethics and morals, on into law and then into religion, until the entire world has been relativized by the end of the twentieth century. This has been one gigantic experiment testing whether or not man can live without absolutes.[8]

That is what has been happening in the twentieth and twenty-first centuries. We cannot blame it on Albert Einstein. He was as appalled as I hope you are. When he saw that his theory was being spread into every conceivable kind of discipline, he said, "Relativity is for physics, not ethics," and that is something I hope in the twenty-first century that we will finally grasp. By the way, if you want a quote from Einstein to repeat whenever you have the opportunity to do so, I recommend using the above observation. If you cannot think of something to say sometime, you could just say this: "You know Albert Einstein said, 'Relativity is for physics, not ethics.'" Just dump it into any conversation. I guarantee it will not lie there.

---

[8] Paul Johnson, *Modern Times* (New York, NY: HarperCollins, 1983).

Of course, God is the ultimate absolute. For those who say there are no absolutes, this is a veiled attempt to cover up their atheism. When people talk about moral relativity, they are covering up their atheism. God is the ultimate absolute, and God's laws are ultimate absolute laws, and they cannot be broken; they cannot be ignored, and God is more than able to call people into account for what they have done with them. Everyone reading this book will one day account for how they have dealt with those laws.

We in the twenty-first century are still being negatively impacted by what happened in the previous hundred years. Of course, the twentieth century was softened up by the voices of a trio of ungodliness.

Karl Marx, who stated that man is controlled not by the absolutes of God, but by economic factors; Sigmund Freud, who said that man is controlled by sexual desires and not by the laws of God; and Friedrich Nietzsche, who said that God is dead, and there are no absolute laws; and therefore the only thing that controls man is the quest for power— man and superman, and man is determined to become superman and to replace God.

So what happened? They denied the law of God. Did they break themselves?

Look at the Soviet "disunion." Here we have utter chaos of every sort. They are in the midst of a depression that would make the 1930s in America look like "Good Times Are Here Again." Total chaos reigns in that nation. I remember being in one of the squares in Russia and seeing one of the statues of Karl Marx that someone had put a rope around and yanked from its place on its pedestal. Here he was face down, broken, upon the concrete. Yes, I think that Karl has destroyed himself and those that followed him.

What about Sigmund Freud? He is passé in psychological circles today. He also created utter chaos with his views and brought about a sexual revolution the effects of which have brought great ill and suffering upon our society and the world.

And then there is Friedrich Nietzsche and his "man and superman." Of course, this quest to be your own God is what is behind all humanism, which would elevate man into the position of God. It is behind all of the New Age religions, which are based on a quest to become God. What about Nietzsche? Well, when last seen he was being led away to the insane asylum. I do not think he was thinking very clearly about the issues any more. He, too, destroyed himself.

CIVIL LAWS

You cannot destroy or break the Law of God; you can only break yourself upon it. So let us consider this so that we may more fully understand the nature of this Law that has been given to us by God in the Old Testament. In the Law that was given to us at Sinai, there were three different kinds of laws. There were, first of all, the civil laws for

Israel. Israel in the Old Testament was different than any nation had ever been before. There was one legislator in Zion and that was God. Israel was what is called a theocracy, and God was the only person in charge. There was no Parliament—the Sanhedrin was a court (the Supreme Court of Israel), and its only job was to interpret the meaning of the Law that God had given.

The civil laws are easily recognized in the Old Testament because they always contain a temporal punishment that consisted either in financial recompense to those who had been robbed or harmed, or stripes or stoning —death. I think it is worth our consideration to note that there were no prisons in Old Testament Israel. Oh, the Babylonians, the Assyrians, and the Romans had prisons. They are sometimes mentioned, but there is no mention of any Israeli prison. Crime was dealt with in an instant manner in ancient Israel—much more peremptorily than it is today.

Those were the civil laws. What happened to them? When the theocracy of Israel was destroyed by Rome in 70 A.D., the civil laws disappeared with them. Now they have no use other than a general guide for all nations in forming their own laws. Since we are not theocracies and we do have a legislature to make laws, they provide only general guidance for that.

CEREMONIAL LAWS

Secondly, there were the ceremonial laws. There was the sin offering and the trespass offering and all the various offerings and sacrifices of the entire sacrificial system. In fact, the sacrificial system was completely ceremonial. These laws were all given at Sinai, and all of them simply foreshadowed the Christ, the Messiah that was to come. When the Substance came, the shadows disappeared. This is why we did not ask you to bring a sacrifice—a lamb, a chicken, or a dove—for your sins this week because the sacrifice has already been made. All of those were simply prefiguring that great One that was to come. As John the Baptist said when he saw Jesus, *"Behold! The Lamb of God who takes away the sin of the world"* (John 1:29). When Christ came and died and rose again, the ceremonial law disappeared. That is why we do not celebrate a Passover or sacrifice offering or sin offering on Sundays. It is gone. It is done.

MORAL LAWS

However, what about the moral law subsumed in the Ten Commandments? All of the moral laws of the Bible can be placed under one or another of those commandments. This is a reflection of the moral nature of God himself, and as such, will never pass away. That is why we find frequent references to the moral laws in the New Testament. When

Paul, in the third chapter of Romans, sums up what could easily be said as one of the most complete explanations of the Christian Gospel, how does he end up? He concludes by saying, *"Do we then make void the law through faith?"* (Romans 3:31).

Now there are some today who would say, "Yes, and amen, brother. We get rid of it. We do not need the law. We do not need to follow it. That is gone. All we need is Christ." That is not what Paul said. I hope all of you know what he said. He said, "Let it not be," or "God forbid." As the text in the King James says, *"Then do we then make the law void through faith? God forbid; yea, we establish the law"* (3:31).

As the Old Testament promised, the commandments of God, the Law of God, would one day be written upon the fleshly tablets of the heart, and so now they are. They become the guide for a Christian whose great desire, having been saved by grace through faith alone, is now to please his Savior. What can he do?

The word "law" in Greek is the word "nomos". Those who are against the Law, those who say that the law has no place at all in the Christian life, are called antinomians (against the law). They say we are saved by grace through faith, and now we do whatever we want. Interestingly, the first heresy trial ever conducted in America was for the sin of antinomianism.

Dr. Kennedy told me once that he would stand up in front of various groups that he was speaking to about the Law, defending this view that we are talking about, and he would ask this question: "Having accepted Jesus Christ and been saved by His grace, is it not your desire now to please Christ and to show your love to Him out of gratitude?"

"Oh, absolutely," the people would say. Then he would ask this question: "Can you name one thing that you can possibly do that would please God other than obeying His commandments?" There was always a roaring silence. There is nothing.

God makes it very clear that He does not want us inventing things to do to please Him. He says, *"Who has required this from your hand, to trample My courts?"* (Isaiah 1:12). Do not invent some works of some super arrogation, or something you think you can do beyond what God has called you to do. You will never begin to do everything God has commanded you to do, let alone start adding on things that He is not.

Finally, one night, Dr. Kennedy was speaking to a group, and a man raised his hand and said, "I have something."

Dr. Kennedy said, "Wonderful! What is it?"

He said, "Love God."

"Surely you jest. Are you not aware of the fact that Jesus Christ summed up the first table of the Law by saying, *"You shall love the Lord your God with all your*

28

heart, with all your soul, and with all your mind. This is the first and great commandment. And the second is like it, You shalt love your neighbor as yourself" (Matthew 22:37-39). No, Jesus did not say, "If you love Me, forget My commandments," did He? He said, *"If you love Me, keep My Commandments"* (John 14:15).

The bit and the bridle are used to tame a wild stallion, but may I remind you that the bit and the bridle are used to guide a tame horse to go in the direction its owner would have it to go. So we who love the Lord, who are saved by grace through faith alone, should desire to please Him in all that we do. This is the purpose of the moral Law today. It is a guide for the Christians to enable us to show our love and gratitude for Christ.

It is not an obedience of slavish fear, like a Roman slave who fears the sting of the taskmaster's whip. It is the obedience of a loving son to his father, whose desire is to please the one who has begotten him, who has reared him, who has cared for him, and who loves him. David said, *"Oh, how I love Your law! It is my meditation all the day."* (Psalm 119:97). Is that your attitude towards the Law?

Remember that keeping the Law has nothing to do with obtaining salvation. It only has to do with how we express our gratitude for it. It has been well said that all of the religions of the world can be expressed in two simple single syllables. All the pagan religions of the world basically say one thing: Do. Do this and don't do that. Only Christianity says: Done! It is done. The last words of Christ before commending His soul to the Father were: "It is finished." "It is done." "It is paid for." "Tetelestai!"[9] "It is enough."

There is nothing to do to obtain our salvation, because Christ has done it all. William Culbertson said that every pagan religion in the world sings this hymn: "Something in my hands I bring."[10] Only Christianity sings: "Nothing in my hands I bring. Only to the Cross I cling."

What is in your hands as you approach God? Salvation is by grace alone, but grace is very difficult for people to understand for the simple reason that the world does not operate by grace. The world operates by a quid pro quo; tit for tat; this for that; so much work, so much pay; by justice. This is all that the world knows, and so people come to God thinking that they are going to get justice.

I am reminded of that famous trial in 1953 when Julius and Ethel Rosenberg were found guilty of giving our atomic secrets to the Soviet Union. By the way, they funneled many other secrets, including the secret for the first jet engine, which they channeled so quickly to the Soviets that when the Korean War broke out, that very

---

[9] Literally translated the word tetelestai means, "It is finished." The Greek-English lexicon by Moulton and Milligan says this: "Receipts are often introduced by the phrase [sic] tetelestai, usually written in an abbreviated manner..." (p. 630). The connection between receipts and what Christ accomplished would have been quite clear to John's Greek-speaking readership; it would be unmistakable that Jesus Christ had died to pay for their sins.

[10] Quote attributed to Dr. William Culbertson, President of Moody Bible Institute from 1948 to 1971.

same year the Soviets had jet-powered MIGS, while we had not even built planes with our own jet engines yet. That was how efficient the Rosenberg's were at channeling secrets.

The Rosenberg's were tried, found guilty, and sentenced to death. Their lawyer said to Judge Kaufman after the verdict was in, "Your honor, all my clients ask for is justice."

Judge Kaufman replied, "What your clients have asked for, this court has given them. What you really mean is that they are asking for mercy. This court is not empowered to grant that," and they died in the electric chair.

Dear friend, we have not given secrets to the enemy, I trust, but every one of us is a traitor. We have rebelled against the most high God and the government of the kingdom of Heaven. We are guilty of breaking all of His laws, violating His earth, killing His Son. There is no doubt about the outcome of the trial, for Christ has already told us. You need not hold your breath to see how you will do in that Great Assize, the final judgment. Here is the verdict. It is already in. "You are condemned already." That is justice, and there is no appeal.

The Good News is that the court is empowered to grant mercy because God Almighty has given His own Son to endure the justice, to pay the just penalty, to suffer infinitely in our stead. For all of those who will come empty-handed, abandoning all trust in their own goodness, piety, or merit and cling to that Cross, the mercy is granted, because Christ has died that we who trust in Him may be spared.

Have you come before that court confessing yourself guilty as charged? Or are you still pretending some goodness or innocence of your own. "Guilty as charged, O Lord. I stand before Thee as a guilty sinner, having violated in thought and word and deed every commandment and am worthy of nothing but Thy just condemnation. But Lord, by faith I place my trust in Christ, and I accept His free promise of everlasting life and pardon and adoption into His family and the granting of His name, a place in His will, an inheritance of Paradise." That is the wonder of grace, and it is that and that alone by which we may be saved.

CONCLUSION

To hear the words, "Well done," at the end of our lives, it goes without saying that first we must be saved by God's grace. Secondly, contrary to many false teachings today, we do need to obey God's law. Next, we look at God's guidance in our lives, living a life that is pleasing to the Lord.

3

A God-Guided Life

(Go Where He Says To Go)

"My son, do not forget my law, but let your heart keep my commands...Bind them around you neck, write them on the tablet of your heart...Trust in the Lord with all your heart, and lean not on your own understanding; in all your ways acknowledge Him, and He shall direct your paths."

Proverbs 3:1, 3, 5, & 6

As the sun settled over the moors of Scotland, the fog hung thickly on the ground, obscuring completely the way of the young man who tried to thread his way across this great expanse of wilderness. He was doing pretty well until he tripped on an extended root coming out from a great tree, and he fell with a thump flat on his face. He was not amused.

He went to push himself up and brush himself off when he discovered there was nothing to push off of. And a careful examination with his fingers revealed that he was but inches from a precipice which he later discovered went hundreds of feet down. He stood tremblingly to his feet and said later that he felt that there was a hand on his shoulder —a hand which had saved his life. He knew from that moment on that he must follow the leading of that hand.

That hand led that young man across the sea to Columbia Theological Seminary, and all the way to the chaplaincy of the Senate of the United States. That man, of course, was Peter Marshall. *A Man Called Peter* was the name of the book and the motion picture made about him. A man who learned early on in his life the reality of the guidance of God—a man who lived a God-guided life.

GUIDANCE

Guidance. Do you need it? It is interesting that there are some people who call themselves Christians that do not seem to think they do. Whereas, on the other hand, there are many Christians who are so obsessed with it that they are extremely troubled because they do not know how to find God's will and guidance for their lives. Do you fit into one of those categories?

Well, let me say, dear friend, that every one of us is desperately in need of guidance, even though you may not think so. Andy Stanley said, "Everybody ends up somewhere in life. A few people end up somewhere on purpose."[11] The goal of most people's lives is to arrive at

---

[11] Andy Stanley, *Visioneering* (Sisters, OR: Multnomah Publishers, 1999).

death safely. Is that your goal? Oh, you might get through life—everybody does, one way or the other. But that does not mean that you are going to accomplish anything of any eternal worth in the sight of Christ. For without Him, He told us, we can do nothing. And I am thoroughly convinced that there are multitudes of church members whose lives really never amount to much because they have never really sought the guidance of God. How about you?

BORN TO BE LED

Did you ever think about the fact that we were born to be led? Now that sort of goes cross-grain for many of us because there are many people who would much prefer to think of themselves as leaders than the led. But if we are Christians, we are born to be led because we are sheep—and that is what you do with sheep, you lead them. And we all profess such (paraphrase): "The Lord is my Shepherd; I shall not want...He leads me to green pastures...to still waters..."[12] If the Lord is our Shepherd and we are His sheep, then we were built to be led.

I was in the Middle East, and was driving down to see the baptism sight of Jesus. There are many tribes of nomads that you can see as you are going down into the canyon where the Jordan River is. As I am watching this one particular group, I notice that there is a great flock of

---

[12] Psalms 23.

35

animals with a man right in the middle. Half of the animals were in front of him, and half of the animals were behind him; and they were all moving gradually up the hill. Can you guess which animals are in front and which are behind? Here is a hint: the ones in the front are not sheep. They are, in fact, goats. The shepherd carries two long switches that he constantly whips at them, because that is the only way you can get a goat to move anywhere. Goats will not follow anybody, anywhere, at any time.

The sheep are behind him, just moseying along, following the shepherd. That is how you know the difference. The goats are in the front and have to be whipped to be driven while the sheep are behind following peacefully.

That's the way it is in church, isn't it? Why there are some people, all you have to do is just hint at what the Lord would want them to do, and they are doing it with alacrity. Others, it would take a two-by-four and a truck to move them one inch off of dead center. Do you follow, or must you be driven? Are you a sheep, or are you a goat? I would remind you that Christ described that last great day as a time when He will divide the sheep from the goats and place the sheep on the one hand and the goats on the other. And say to these, *"Enter into the joy of your lord"* (Matthew 25:23), and to the goats, *"Depart from me..."* (Matthew 7:23). So I say again: Are you born to be led? Are you following Christ? Is He your Shepherd? Do you really feel the need, the longing, for His guidance?

Well, may I say that the more devout a Christian is, the more deeply he feels that need. It is enshrined in so many of our familiar hymns. How about:

"All the way my Savior leads me; What have I to ask beside? Can I doubt His tender mercy, Who through life has been my guide?"[13]

"He leadeth me, O blessed thought. O words with heavenly comfort fraught. What-e'er I do, where-e'er I be, Still 'tis God's hand that leadeth me."[14]

"Jesus Savior, pilot me, Over life's tempestuous sea; Unknown waves before me roll, Hidden rock and treacherous shoal; Chart and compass came from Thee: Jesus, Savior, pilot me."[15]

"Because the Lord is my Shepherd, I have everything that I need. He lets me rest in meadows green, And leads me beside the quiet stream."[16]

---

[13] Fanny Crosby, in *Brightest and Best*, by Robert Lowry and W. Howard Doane (New York: Biglow & Main, 1875), number 65.

[14] Joseph H. Gilmore, 1862.

[15] Edward Hopper, in *The Sailor's Magazine* (1871) and *The Baptist Praise Book* (1871). The nautical theme reflects Hopper's ministry at the Church of the Sea and Land in New York City, where he met sailors from around the world.

[16] Christopher Walker.

"Lead on, O King Eternal, The day of march has come."[17]

These and many, many more indicate the deep longing of the devout heart for the guidance and leading of God. Do you feel that in your own life? The closer you come to Christ, the more acutely you will be aware of your need for that guidance.

Second, may I point out that God promises to provide it in His Word; over and over again we see that God has promised to provide that for us.

"For this God is our God forever and ever: He will be our guide, even to death" (Psalm 48:14).

"You will guide me with Your counsel, and afterward receive me to glory" (Psalm 73:24).

"And He led them forth by the right way, that they might go to a city for a dwelling place" (Psalm 107:7).

"To him [said Jesus, the Good Shepherd] the doorkeeper opens, and the sheep hear his voice: and he calls his own sheep by name and leads them out" (John 10:3).

"However, when He, the Spirit of truth, has come, He will guide you into all truth" (John 16:13).

---

[17] Ernest W. Shurtleff, 1888. He wrote this hymn for the graduation ceremony at Andover Theological Seminary, where he was a member of the class of 1888.

And then, that categorical description of what is a son of God or child of God. It is non-technical, non-theological. Anybody should be able to understand it, but it is very true. Said Paul in Romans 8:14, *"For as many as are led by the Spirit of God, these are sons of God."* How wonderful that is that God has provided such guidance. Are you being led by the Spirit of God?

Not only does God promise us His guidance, but also He provides that guidance and has done so from the very beginning. He led Enoch on a walk that took him all the way to Heaven. He led Noah into an ark and through the great deluge. He led Abram up from Ur of the Chaldees to Canaan. He led Joseph from a dungeon to the throne of Egypt. He led Moses through the wilderness and back to Egypt to lead His people forth. He led David from keeping the sheep to sitting upon the throne of Israel. And He leads His people evermore. He has led them and continues to lead them down through the ages.

Have you experienced that guidance in your life? The apostle Paul most certainly did. And it is a very interesting story that he describes in Acts 16. You remember when they said that they assayed to go into Asia, and the Holy Spirit forbade them. And then they decided to turn the other way and go into Bithynia, *"but the Spirit did not permit them"* (vs. 7), and they were compelled to go to Troas. And there at Troas, Paul received the vision in which he saw a man standing across the water saying, from Macedonia,

"Come over...and help us" (vs. 9). And Paul took the Gospel for the first time to Europe, and thus to most of us, led by the Spirit of God.

But I want you to understand one thing about the leading of God's Spirit. It is not always easy or comfortable. What Paul experienced was running into one wall after another, one obstacle after another as God led him, so he could later say, that we are constrained by the love of Christ into His will. He was not buoyed up and carried along by some wave of happy circumstances, but rather, he struggled constantly against one obstacle after another in an effort to transcend the limitations that circumstances seemed to place upon him. And he continued this struggle throughout all of His life because he believed that in, and behind, and under all of those struggles there was the hand of God leading him inexorably toward God's glorious consummation for his life.

Is that the conviction of your heart? I know that certainly in my life it hasn't been a matter of being carried on a wave of happy circumstances, but it has been confronting one obstacle after another in an effort to transcend the limitations which circumstances seem to place on my life, because I have had the deep conviction that God has been leading me all along. I know from my own personal experience.

As I look back, I see that it was the hand of God that led me to the Omaha Gospel Tabernacle.[18] As I lived it, I can remember the circumstances seeming logical and natural—not painless certainly, but sensible. I had seen my best friend Mike change to a more peaceful, happy person, and I had no explanation for it except that he was going to that church. So, I decided to check it out the next Sunday to see with my own eyes what influenced this miraculous change in his life.

During the week before, I had a young man working for me named Scott (who had been telling me about Jesus since he got the job) give me a CD. Now Scott gave me a CD of Christian music almost every time I saw him (the persistence of Christians, I tell you!), and I would throw them into the corner of the studio which most of the time broke them or cracked their cases. But he was never discouraged. He just kept giving me those CDs. That week, Scott gave me a CD by Steven Curtis Chapman; and for once, I did not throw it into the corner. I slipped it into the CD player, and it went directly to track three. I thought, "That's strange," so I took it out, cleaned it, and put it back in. Track three came up again, so I gave up and decided to listen to it. It was a beautiful song about the still, small voice of God. I was thoroughly shocked—the book I had recently been reading was on the very same topic. When I

---

[18] It was named the Omaha Gospel Tabrenacle when I first came to know about the church. The name was changed to Christ Community Church and is part of the C & MA.

walked in the door of the church on Sunday morning, you want to guess what the sermon was on? The still, small voice of God.

I came to the conclusion that the still, small voice was trying to tell me something, so I went back to the church the following Monday morning to find out what God was trying to say to me. I met a pastor there named Tom Stebbins, and he asked me two great questions and shared the Gospel in a way I had never heard before. I gave my heart to Jesus that very day, and I was changed. Not long after, my wife Ann heard the Gospel and gave her heart to Christ as well.

From there, God grew us up in Him, teaching us to trust Him more and more until finally, He called us to leave our home and follow Him into full-time Christian service.

I am not so sure that it was all that clear when it was happening; but now, in retrospect, it seems perfectly, crystal clear.

How do we discover the will of God and the guidance of God for our lives? I think, first of all, we need to realize our need of it, because it does not matter how strong, or how wise or how fast you are, if you are lost in the middle of a vast wilderness, you are not going to come out unscathed. And we most certainly will drive our lives into the ditch if God is not giving us guidance. I think one of the first things any smart Christian will do is say, "Lord, you drive"—and relinquish the steering wheel of his or her life to the Savior.

Third, we need to believe that divine guidance is available. We have all the promises of God and all of the provision of that guidance down through the entire recorded history of the world to strengthen us in that belief.

And fourth, we need to pray daily for it. Dr. Kennedy told me once that every morning, before his feet even touched the ground, he would say this prayer, "Guide me, O Thou Great Jehovah, Pilgrim through a barren land." I have tried to adopt this into my own life as well. May I encourage you that before your feet hit the floor every morning, pray, "Guide me, O Thou Great Jehovah, Pilgrim through a barren land." There are many snares and many temptations and many difficulties out there. We definitely need the guidance of God.

Fifth, we need to surrender our wills to that guidance. There are many people that have the idea that their plan for their life is better than God's plan. I would ask you: Whose plan for your life are you working out? Most people have "thunk it up" themselves. And usually, it is very fruitless. It accomplishes nothing in the overall scheme of things.

As Christ said, *"Without me, you can do nothing"* (John 15:5). Oh, you might manage to get yourself from here to a grave—no great accomplishment. But as far as accomplishing anything that is going to have lasting and eternal significance without the guidance of

43

God, you will never really make it. We need to surrender our will, but many people are afraid that the will of God is going to be harsh and unloving.

The late Bill Bright said one time that since he traveled a great deal when his children were growing up, he did not see them all that often. But whenever he would come home, he would say to his two little boys, "Well, guys, what would you like to do?" Well, there was always one thing that they would like to do—they liked to get down on the living room floor and wrestle with their daddy. And so, that is what they would do. One time he thought to himself, "I wonder what would happen if I came home and heard my kids say, 'Daddy, what would you like to do?'"

"What would I say? I would say, 'Aha, now I've got you, and now you're going to have spinach three times a day, and no more ice cream. You're going to do homework six hours a day and mow the lawn every other day.'" He said, "I wouldn't have said that. I would be so amazed, I probably would say, 'Well, guys, what I'd like is an ice cream cone. Would either of you like to go with me?' And when we got home, I would probably say, 'Why don't we get down on the rug and wrestle?'"

God's banner over us is love—an infinite love, and His plan for our life is far more loving and satisfying and fulfilling than any plan that we would ever know. I would urge you to yield yourself to that and discover the full wonder of that love.

Sixth, we need to be patient. God does not always make His will known to us as quickly as we would like and lead us in a way that solves all of the problems we have. What problem are you struggling with right now? Do you need a new job? Do you need a new car? Do you need a new house? You need... who knows what?

God knows about it, but God is not always going to reveal the answer to you as soon as you would like. Why not? Because it is in such testings as these that our faith grows. Why is it that weight lifting or isometrics cause muscles to grow? Because it is the tension, the stress, the pressure that the muscle is under that causes it to grow. And the same is true of our faith. It is only when we face difficulties that we cannot transcend on our own that we need to trust the Lord, and in trusting the Lord, learn to trust Him more.

Those of you who have walked for a good many years down the path with Christ have learned through many, many experiences that He can be trusted, because you have faced one crisis after another after another all of your life—and you have found that He has been faithful. And how wondrous that is to find His faithfulness—to find that no matter what happens, that He is going to be there to bring you through it. And you learn to trust Him more. But if He answered all of your prayers immediately, just because you started out so impatiently, like the little child, who says, "Gimme, gimmee, gimmee. Daddy, I want..." and wanted everything right now, you would find yourself completely at home in a society that wants instant gratification for everything. Doesn't that sound rather familiar to our society at present? We need to learn to be patient.

In Numbers 9, it tells about how the pillar of cloud by day and the pillar of fire by night hovered over the Tabernacle. And when the pillar moved, the people of God moved; and when the pillar stopped, the people stopped. Simple enough. You would think that would be enough to tell a story. But then the pillar moved, we are told, and stopped, and they waited for a day or two...or many days. And then the pillar moved, and they moved. And then the pillar stopped, and they stopped; and they waited for a few days. And the pillar moved, and they moved. And the pillar stopped, and they stopped. And the pillar moved, and they moved. And the pillar stopped, and they stopped. And you wonder why in the world does the inspired writer keep repeating this. Finally, you get the point. He is trying to tell us that God wants us to follow His guidance. And remember this: the manna only fell where the pillar lodged.

You can say, "Well, I think we ought to go that-a-way. This pillar is driving me crazy." Maybe even get some people to follow you. That is called a schism. One thing you will discover: There is no manna out there. Now, some of you may be experiencing that in your own life—the manna isn't falling. Oh, that is not to say you're not getting enough to eat, but the manna isn't falling on your soul. You do not find that satisfaction. You do not discover that fulfillment that you looked for. You do not find the joy you had hoped for in these wonderful plans that you conceived. Maybe you ought to check and see which way the pillar went—what God really intended for your life. Are you really following Him?

Someone once said that we do a lot better at "fellowship" than we do at "followship." I think there is a lot of truth in that. We need to realize our need of guidance, and we need to pray daily for it. When you wake up in the morning, before you place your foot on the carpet, say, "Guide me, O Thou great Jehovah, Pilgrim through a barren land," and seek that guidance from Him.

As David said, *"Show me Your ways, O Lord"* (Psalm 25:4). Surrender our wills to it, knowing that His will for our life is the best, and patiently wait for God to reveal that will.

Lastly, we need to believe that we are being guided. The Bible says that He will guide us continually in our lives. He cares what happens to us. He is willing to guide us.

I once heard a story about a man in New England. I do not remember what state he was in. But he was traveling along in his car, and he was going to some city—Granite City or whatever it might be. And he came to a fork in the road. And the sign for one road said, "Granite City" this way. The other sign said "Granite City" that way. And he was utterly perplexed. As he stopped his car, he noticed a farmer out on a tractor. He got out of his car and walked across the broken field. Finally the farmer saw him, stopped his plow, and said, "Yeah?" The man responded, "Excuse me, sir, does it make any difference which road I take to get to Granite City?" "Not to me, it don't."

Well, a lot of people think that is the way God feels; but He cares about us, and He promises to guide us continually. We need to realize that He is faithful, and we are being guided every day of our lives.

CONCLUSION

Consider again, Peter Marshall. At the end of his ministry, he said as he looked back upon his life, with all of the obstacles and difficulties, and all of the decisions that he had to make, which sometimes seemed so hard, that he did not really know what the will of God was for him. But he prayed and sought that will and made the decision. And he said, "Now, as I look back, I can see that the hand of God was on my shoulder leading me every step of the way."

"Guide me, O Thou Great Jehovah, Pilgrim through a barren land."[19] Dear friend, be wise. Seek daily the guidance of God for your life.

---

[19] William Williams, *Halleluiah* (Bristol, England: 1745). Translated from Welsh to English by Peter Williams, *Hymns on Various Subjects* (Carmarthen, Wales: 1771); Williams published another English translation in *Lady Huntingdon's Collection*, circa 1772.

4

He That Perseveres

(Secure Your Heart)

"But he who endures to the end shall be saved."

Matthew 24:13

Jesus Christ said, *"He who endures to the end shall be saved"* (Matthew 24:13). These words have caused many Christians to be troubled and to cast about in their minds trying to understand their meaning. How should they fit them into their doctrinal understanding of the Scripture? How should they fit them in with that doctrine known as the perseverance of the saints? The eternal security of the believer is a doctrine many have had difficulties with.

There have been those who have emphasized almost entirely the verses of the Scripture that talk about our security and our safety. There have been others who have emphasized, almost completely, the fact of the warnings or admonitions in the Scripture. Sometimes, it seems that it is just a matter of which group of texts we want to look at— that there is some sort of antinomy that exists between them. But of course, if we believe the Bible is the Word of God, then obviously both groups of texts are true.

It is both true that he that perseveres to the end shall be saved, and also that no man snatches them out of His hand. The Scripture says, *"My Father who has given them to Me, is greater than all; and no one is able to snatch them out of My Father's hand"* (John 10:29). Presbyterians of the Calvinistic persuasion have often been accused by those of the Armenian view of ignoring the warnings or admonitions of Scripture and fixing our minds only upon the promises of safety and security. There is, to a degree, some element of truth in that, I am sure, especially in some spheres more than others. Certainly it is not true among the great theologians and commentators of the Reformed faith, but among particular Christians no doubt you can often find that this is the case.

Since we are dealing with matters of the practical life of the Christian, I am going to approach this subject of the admonitions of the Scriptures, the warnings of the Scriptures, as they apply to our daily life. There are two aspects to the doctrine of the perseverance of the saints: the divine aspect and the human aspect. There is the divine promise of security to those who truly believe, and there is the human responsibility to take heed, watch, and to endure to the end. Both of these are real. Both of them are serious. Both of them are to be considered carefully by all true believers.

THE HUMAN ASPECT

Let us consider some of the admonitions of the Scripture. We are told that if we keep His commandments, we abide in His love. Christ says, *"If anyone does not abide in Me, he is cast out as a branch and is withered; and they gather them and throw them into the fire, and they are burned"* (John 15:6). We are His friends, He says, if we do whatsoever He commands us. Paul says, *"If indeed you continue in the faith, grounded and steadfast, and are not moved away from the hope of the gospel..."* (Colossians 1:23). We are warned not only by Christ but also by all the writers of the New Testament that we are to be faithful unto death, and Christ will give us a crown of life. There are earnest warnings that call us to walk the straight and narrow path, which appears to be flanked on either side by the abyss. We are told that the ancient apostasy of Israel in the desert, where multitudes fell and their carcasses were bleached in the desert sun, happened as examples to us and that we are to heed these admonitions.

We are told in Romans that if God spared not the natural branches, Israel, but severed them and grafted in the wild branch of the Gentiles, that we are not to boast but to be careful lest we, too, also be cut off. We are told by the author of Hebrews: *"Beware, brethren, lest there be in any of you an evil heart of unbelief in departing from the living God"* (3:12). We are not to refuse to hear Him that speaks to us through His Word; we are not to quench the Spirit of

God. We are told that if we deny Him, He will also deny us. The Apostle Paul tells us of some who have made shipwrecks of their faith. In the New Testament alone we read about Hymenaeus and Alexander and Demas and Philetus. *"...for Demas has forsaken me, having loved this present world, and has departed..."* (2 Timothy 4:10), said Paul.

We are warned of those who have erred from the truth; of the gross example of Judas, who betrayed His Lord after being elevated in a high position as an Apostle, who hanged himself and went to his own place. We are warned in Hebrews of those who crucify afresh the Son of God and put Him to an open shame. We are told that those who sin willfully after having a knowledge of the truth, that there remains no sacrifice for sin *"...who has trampled the Son of God underfoot, counted the blood of the covenant by which he was sanctified a common thing, and insulted the Spirit of grace"* (Hebrews 10:29). Instead, they have this to look forward to: *"a certain fearful expectation of judgment, and fiery indignation which will devour the adversaries"* (Hebrews 10:27). These passages and scores of others from the Scriptures cannot be ignored by any Christian who would take seriously the Word of God. God did not put those passages in the Bible for naught. He put them there for warning, for our admonition. We need to heed them.

In my lifetime, I have seen numbers of people who have begun well. They have made a good profession of their faith; they have been baptized; they have become members of the church; and they have served in this activity or that. Then suddenly, but more often slowly, they have faded away. There are those who have even been officers in a church, those who have taught Sunday School, and those who have been involved in numerous programs, which now never darken the door of God's house. They are not found among His saints. They do not turn to Him in His Word. They want nothing to do with the things of Christ. Like Demas, they have loved this present world and departed from Him. There have always been those who fall away; they exist in church. They exist all the way back to that very first group of twelve, namely Judas, as previously mentioned.

If that is true, then it also must be true that among those reading this book, it is possible that there exists some who one day will be found in that same category. That is, that one or two or five or ten years from now they will no longer be found among the saints of God. They will have turned away like Demas. Whether it will be the love of the world, or some other sin, I cannot say. But I know this: there are some church-goers who a few years hence will have completely apostatized from the Christian faith. As the Scripture says, *"Therefore let him who thinks he stands take heed lest he fall"* (1 Corinthians 10:12). That is a long,

long fall, and it has everlasting consequences. You say, "That will never happen to me." It is just to such an attitude that these words of Scripture are written. *"...work out your own salvation with fear and trembling"* (Philippians 2:12). Watch, pray, take heed—for it is only that one who endures to the end who shall be saved.

How does Satan accomplish this? He has various wiles —numerous stratagems and ploys that he has used. There is the one where a person becomes upset with something that somebody said to them. Can you imagine a person trading his soul for that? Yet I have seen it happen numerous times. Somebody has said something to a person, and they have let that lodge in their soul and begin to fester. It grows and it grows and it grows and it becomes the biggest thing in the world. They munch on it at night, "How could that person have said that to me? Who do they think they are?" Their whole body and soul is poisoned by these thoughts. Gradually, they fade away.

I have seen numerous people who have made a profession of faith. They have become very zealous. They have come not only on Sunday morning, but Sunday night. They have also come Wednesday night to a prayer meeting. They have been found every time the door of the church was opened. And yet, they have become upset with something that someone has said; they have a grievance, which they allow to fester. Soon they are not found in prayer meetings because it is hard to pray when they feel that way. They do not come on Sunday night because they just do not want to any more. As for Sunday School—well "that person" is in their class. So they just come on Sunday morning. After all, that is enough isn't it? The reading of the Word of God becomes very grievous because it seems that every time they open the Bible, God is talking about being reconciled and forgiving those that hurt them. So the Scriptures are closed and begin to gather dust. Soon, they only attend occasionally, and at last, they have slipped away completely. I can think of numbers of people who have followed that whole syndrome right to the end.

There are others who begin well; they make a profession of faith, they become regular in the church, and yet, something happens in the world. Some sin in their daily life, something in their business isn't right. They know it is wrong, but they continue to do it. Maybe it is a moral issue. Maybe they are becoming involved with someone in a way they shouldn't become involved and the same cooling down process begins to take place. They find that everything about God—His church, His people, His Word, prayer—only conflicts with this sin which now they are holding onto with all of their might. They have a choice: either repent of that sin and give it up, or else give up the Word, the Church, prayer, and the Lord. Some of them will give up the latter. I have seen that happen many times. I know those that years ago were faithful in the church who have not darkened its doors, nor the doors of any church for years. Some of you, a few years hence, may be found in their numbers. *"Take heed while you stand lest you fall"* (1 Corinthians 10:12).

THE DIVINE ASPECT

What is the way in which these promises of God relate to these warnings and admonitions? For on the other side, we are told, *"I will never leave you nor forsake you...[nothing] shall be able to separate us from the love of God which is in Christ Jesus...I give them eternal life, and they shall never perish...being confident of this very thing, that He who has begun a good work in you will complete it until the day of Jesus Christ"* (Hebrews 13:5; Romans 8:39; John 10:28; Philippians 1:6). We believe that salvation is of grace and totally of grace. From the beginning to the end, from eternity to eternity, it is all of grace. Salvation is of faith that it might be of grace, and it is of grace that it might be of God. Salvation is by God.

What, then, do we have to do with it? We are told in the Scripture that we are to repent of our sins. We are to place our trust in the crucified Christ for our salvation. If we dig more deeply, we will discover that even repentance and faith are gifts from God. Dr. William Childs Robinson used to say: "God requires repentance and faith that we might be saved. But that which He requires, He also freely gives, that the whole thing may be of grace."[20] Repentance is the work of God, and faith is the work of God. This is the work of God that you believe in Him whom He has sent. *"A servant of the Lord must not quarrel...[but] in humility [correct] those who are in opposition, if God perhaps will grant them repentance"* (2 Timothy 2:24-25).

It is also true in the continuation of the Christian in life. Just as we are commanded to repent and believe, and yet repentance and faith are gifts from God and by His grace, as we are commanded to persevere (to endure to the end), we are also told that it is by His grace that He enables His own to endure; that without that grace we would not endure for so much as a week. Therefore, we have nothing to boast about if we have endured or if we have persevered, because we know that it is entirely due to His grace, which has been operative in us from beginning to end. Salvation is of grace.

The reason, then, for the admonitions and the warnings in light of the fact that it is God that keeps us is well expressed by Charles Hodge, the late Princeton theologian. He said that the reason for these admonitions is that God keeps us not by magical means but by moral means. Therefore, He exhorts, He warns, and He admonishes us. If we deny Him, He will deny us. *"Turn not aside therefrom to the right hand or to the left...Enter by the narrow gate...let him who thinks he stands take heed lest he fall...Watch and pray...Flee [temptation]"* (Joshua 23:6 KJV;

---

[20] Dr. Robinson was a professor at Columbia Theological Seminary from 1926 to 1967.

Matthew 7:13; 1 Corinthians 10:12; Matthew 26:41; 1 Corinthians 6:18)—in order that by moral means, His Spirit, by His grace, will enable us to walk that path which leads unto eternal life.

What, then, shall we say about those who have apparently begun the Christian life and yet apostatized? There is one of two things that could be said: Either they began to be Christians, and they ceased; or they were never truly Christians at all. There are those who opt for either side. It is my conviction and the conviction of the Reformed Faith that the Scripture teaches that this merely demonstrates that they were never true believers at all. The Apostle John makes this plain in the second chapter of his first epistle when he talks about those that have apostatized and went out from among the believers and denied Christ. He said this about them: *"They went out from us, but they were not of us; for if they had been of us, they would have continued with us: but they went out that they might be made manifest, that none of them were of us"* (1 John 2:19).

CONCLUSION

Are you truly one of God's own? Will you be found among His saints five years from now? Ten years from now? The day that you die? How can we know? If we truly trust Him, then we have the assurance first of all through His promise, secondly, through His Holy Spirit which bears witness with our spirit that we are the children of God, and thirdly, through the evidence of those graces to which the promises of God are made. That is, if we truly belong to Christ, we have become new creatures: *"Therefore, if anyone is in Christ, he is a new creation; old things have passed away; behold, all things have become new"* (2 Corinthians 5:17).

A young lady asked me if she really was a Christian because she continued on in sin. I said that God bears witness by the graces given to our life, and that seemed to encourage her, but I reminded her that one of those graces is virtue.

Are you truly one of God's own? Have you turned from your sins to follow Him? If so, then the Christian's attitude should be twofold. To claim the promises of God: *"I will never leave you nor forsake you"* (Hebrews 13:5); to rest in the assurance he has given to us; *"I give them eternal life, and they shall never perish"* (John 10:28). To trust with the same assurance Paul had: *"...being confident of this very thing, that He who has begun a good work in you will complete it until the day of Jesus Christ"* (Philippians 1:6). Also, to take heed to Christ's admonition: *"...he who endures to the end shall be saved"* (Matthew 24:13).

5

Light Always Wins

(Be a Light)

"You are the light of the world. A city that is set on a hill cannot be hidden."

Matthew 5:14

The crowd had gathered from what seemed like everywhere. The city was straining under the weight of all of their needs. This particular night the crowds were packed inside, outside, and everywhere near the temple. They had come to celebrate the Feast of Tabernacles. During this feast there were two great ceremonies: one was the pouring of water (to remember God's provision of water for the people of Israel during their years in the wilderness), and the second was the illumination of the temple (to remember how God had provided a cloud that had offered protection from the extreme heat of the day and a pillar of fire that had offered illumination and heat during the cold desert nights. Without this light, they would have surely perished.)

So here they were, gathered to celebrate the lighting of the immense candelabra in the temple. The crowd murmured with expectation. Priests had made the preparations, climbing ladders and pouring sixty-five liters of highly flammable oil into each of the four vast candelabra. At the right moment, they lit the candelabra and sent light streaming throughout the temple, throughout the courtyard, and out into the streets of Jerusalem. For a moment, time seemed to stand still. The light illuminated faces in wonder. As it flashed down the street, the shopkeepers stopped to stare as night became day in a split second. The crowd silenced with a collective, "Ahhhh."

There in the hush of the amazed crowd a voice was heard. It was the voice of Jesus, and He said the most incredible thing. "I am the light of the world. If you follow Me, you will not be stumbling through the darkness, because you will have the light that leads to life" (based on John 8:12).

What a statement Jesus was making. He was the light of the world. He was the One who had sheltered them during the day and kept them safe at night. He was and is the only One that offers us the ability to walk without stumbling. He is the One that leads us to life eternal.

We live in a day and age when "experts" have many ideas about what people need to live in this country and in this world. And yet, they have no actual answers for the darkness that creeps into our lives. Recent years have seen their share of darkness. We here in the United States are still wounded by the reminder of the terrible tragedy on September 11, 2001 when two airplanes were crashed into the Twin Towers of New York, one airplane into the Pentagon, while yet another crashed into a field. People in Thailand, Indonesia, and throughout Asia have continued to struggle to put their lives back together after the tsunami of 2004. In Sudan in 2010, a massive genocide is taking place with over 300,000 casualties due to famine, disease, and war associated with the slaughtering of the Darfur by the Janjaweed.

And it is not just the darkness that comes from physical challenges and the loss of hope, but also there is a moral darkness that continues to creep into our land. To see it, you need only to look at the movies that Hollywood is forcing on us and celebrating. Read Romans 1, and it is really clear what is going on.

We know more, we have more, and yet we seem to be doing less when it comes to fulfilling the first and last commandments of our Lord and Savior Jesus Christ.

First, Jesus commanded to His disciples (after telling them to repent), *"Follow Me, and I will make you fishers of men"* (Matthew 4:19). Last He said, *"Go into all the world and preach the gospel to every creature"* (Mark 16:15).

How are we doing?

REACHING THE UNREACHED

When we talk about trying to reach people of different cultures with the Gospel of Jesus Christ, we are not just talking about reaching people in distant lands. There are culture shifts happening right now within the millennials and Gen'xers of the United States. I have heard it said that three out of four Gen'xers will never darken a church doorway except for a funeral or wedding. Even within the U.S. adult population, one in three are unchurched, which translates into 65 to 70 million people.[21] The unchurched population in the United States is the largest mission field in the English speaking world and the fifth largest globally.[22]

William Bennett stated, "In many parts of America we have become the kind of place to which civilized countries used to send missionaries."[23]

Where is our passion in all of this? As we saw earlier, many professing Christians do not put their money where their mouth is.

All of us could do better and be more open to the leading of the Holy Spirit. When we look at the culture around us and realize we are called to be salt and light, the

---

[21] Tom Clegg & Warren Bird, *Lost in America* (Loveland, CO: Group Publishing, 2001), 25.

[22] Kent R. Hunter, *Move Your Church Into Action* (Nashville, TN: Abingdon Press, 2000), 12.

[23] William J. Bennett, "Does Honor Have a Future?" The Forrestal Lecture delivered before the United States Naval Academy, November 24, 1997.

task seems overwhelming. But the key for us Christians is to bloom where we are planted and to take advantage of the opportunities God gives us. Unfortunately, many Christians do not look for such opportunities, and the impact on our culture has been devastating.

Our nation's moral compass has gone haywire. Certainly, the Church is partly to blame because too many Christians have bought into the theology of consumerism and the philosophy that you only go around once; therefore, you must get all you can out of life. Nothing really matters, so anything goes.

We are not out there teaching God's rules, so any rule must be man's and therefore arbitrary. Many people feel that rules do not apply to them, or that they can be bent to suit their needs.

In a recent survey conducted by the Josephson Institute of Ethics, they found that:

91 percent of Americans admit to lying regularly to people closest to them;

74 percent steal items when they think they will not be missed;

56 percent say they will drink and drive if they think they can handle it;

55 percent say they would cheat on their spouse;

40 percent confess to using illegal drugs;

30 percent claim they cheat on their taxes;

and 93 percent of adults and teens say that they and nobody else determine what is and isn't moral in their lives.[24]

When we as the Church disengage from the culture, all kinds of bad things happen. In only one day here in America:

3,246 women will have an abortion and 3,445 unmarried women will give birth to a child;

3,110 couples will get divorces;

84 people will commit suicide;

45 people will die of AIDS;

9,260 teenagers will have sex for the first time;

28,206 people will be arrested, 4,274 of them for drug violations;

3,396 households will declare bankruptcy;

411 Americans will convert to the Muslim faith, 872 will become Mormons;

and 8 churches will close their doors for the last time.[25]

And the crazy thing is that we disengage mostly because we do not think people want to hear what we have

---

[24] Bill Bright & John N. Damoose, *Red Sky in the Morning* (Orlando, FL: NewLife Publications, 1998), 153.

[25] Tom Clegg & Warren Bird, 16.

to say about Jesus. Although we do not always believe it, a lot of people are open to the Gospel.

During one of our leadership-training clinics, I took my team out to an outdoor mall in Fresno, California.[26] We approached a girl named Monica. She was waiting for the theater to get out. I asked her two questions: (1) Do you know for sure if you were to die tonight that you would go to be with God in Heaven? She said she hoped so, but did not know. Then I asked her, (2) "Monica, if you were to die tonight and stand before God and He were to say to you, 'Why should I let you into My Heaven,' what would you say?" She answered, "I hope I've done enough good things to get in." As I shared the Gospel, with tears in her eyes, she accepted the free gift of eternal life through Jesus. When we were done and about to leave she said, "Wait a minute. Here's the card from a pastor that I went to see this morning. I was asking him how to get to Heaven, but he did not know. Would you go tell him as well?"

A second story is about a clinic that we did in Salt Lake City during the Olympics, many years ago. The church there had gone through great turmoil as they decided to stop focusing on building the church inside the walls and get out there and engage the community. It sounded like a pretty scary thing to many people in a place like Salt Lake.

---

[26] We, at Evangelism Explosion, conduct leadership-training clinics in the United States (and around the world) and take people out every week witnessing for Jesus. Nationwide in the U.S. we see about 30% of those we share with profess to accept Christ.

In fact, many people left the church when they found out about this new movement to become a witnessing church.

One of the folks on my team was agitated about going out on Tuesday to witness, and I asked her, "Why?" She told me the core issue. She said, "I don't believe that there is anyone here in Salt Lake that wants to hear what we have to say."

We walked out the door and led two high-school boys to Jesus on the doorstep of the church and then went downtown and led a guy named Todd to the Lord, and she was changed. Later, she said, "I just didn't see how open people are to the Gospel."

People are amazingly open. One day my son Josh and I went with a group out to a pretty poor neighborhood to share the Gospel. We had hotdogs and sodas, some kids did a few skits, and we heard a testimony. Then we talked one-on-one with some of the folks that came out. The man we spoke to was named Jerry. Jerry was 81 years old and he was thrilled to hear about and accept Jesus. Right before we left he said, "I've been in this neighborhood for 51 years and you all are the first Christians I remember seeing."

It is easy for us to miss the big picture. It is estimated that 2,000 people die everyday here in the United States and go to an eternity in Hell separated from God. We as Christians would like to see that change. Most of us would like to share the Gospel with others, given the opportunity to do so. We at Evangelism Explosion exist to help Christians share the Gospel with confidence.

So why do so few Christians witness?

I have thought a lot about this, and I am sure I do not know the whole answer. But surely part of it must be that firstly, we have bought into false views of salvation like universalism (the belief that everyone is saved), auto-soteriology (the idea that we are saved by our own works), perhaps we think that we are saved by membership in a particular church, or just by being religious.

Secondly, it is possible that we do not understand our condition or the condition of those that are lost. We are pretty confused over Heaven and Hell, and we are pretty poor judges of our condition. 77% of American's viewed their chances of getting into Heaven as good or excellent.[27] The truth is that no one is saved without Jesus.

Thirdly, we do not understand our obligation before God to achieve His purposes in our lives. We have gotten it into our heads that we are our own. The Bible teaches us that we are not our own; we have been bought with a price.[28] We are stewards of this life and sent by our Master to take His light to everyone. We have forgotten Luke 15 and the parables of the lost sheep, lost coin, and the lost

---

[27] Taken from a 1988 Gallup Poll published at: http://www.gallup.com/poll/11770/eternal-destinations-americans-believe-heaven-hell.aspx.

[28] 1 Corinthians 6:19-20.

son. Here we see the intensity and passion of God for the lost.

Lastly, perhaps we imagine that we ourselves are too small to make a difference.

The reality is that if only one Christian were able to share his or her faith with a non-believer, see that person come to saving faith in Jesus, and then teach that person how to witness as well, within 34 generations of this process, everyone on earth would be reached.

Or, let's look at it another way: If every Christian would learn how to witness, start to pray that God would lead them to one person who would be open to the Gospel, share their faith and see them come to Christ, the Church would double in a very short period of time. If they were included and this process were repeated four times, the job would be done, Jesus would come again, and we can go home. Sound good to you?

It is not only possible; it is relatively easy if we would only be salt and light, get engaged, learn to share our faith, and get out there.

This is a process (as previously mentioned) called Spiritual Multiplication, and it is powerful. Some have started to talk about it recently, but Dr. Kennedy has been talking about it for 50 years. Spiritual Multiplication is the answer from Holy Scripture for reaching our world for Christ. The Apostle Paul laid down the principle 2,000 years ago: *"And the things that you have heard from me among many witnesses, commit these to faithful men who will be able to teach others also"* (2 Timothy 2:2).

AN AWESOME RESPONSIBILITY

It is an awesome responsibility to own a Bible. For the Bible is clear about our responsibility before Almighty God. We have been given two mandates, both tied together and inseparable: The cultural mandate to be salt and the evangelism mandate to be light.

If we will only do what God has placed us here to do, we can shine like the stars forever according to Daniel (12:3). Are you up to it? Maybe you say, "I'm not great enough for such heights." As Admiral William Halsey said, "There aren't any great men. There are just great challenges that ordinary men like you and me are forced by circumstances to meet."[29]

The great challenge and purpose of our lives must be to see this nation and our world reached for Christ, and to see it transformed to the glory of God. It must become unacceptable to us for there to be people alive who have never heard of Jesus. We must be salt and light.

The heartbeat of the Church must be evangelism; all Christians are mandated to share their faith; the world is primed and ready for evangelism; and equipping and

---

[29] Admiral William Frederick Jr. was an American Naval Officer during World War II, 1882 to 1959.

empowering laypeople is the key to reaching the world for Christ.

Moreover, we know the outcome. The bottom line is that we win.

I have read the last chapter of the Book. We win.

It is not hard for light to defeat darkness. Even if the room you are in is pitch black, absolutely dark, without a ray of light coming in, it would only take a small candle to offer light to the very corners of the room.

And so, even in the midst of great difficulty, the light of the Gospel is going forward. Rev. Tom Mangham, EE's VP for Asia, once sent me a note with a picture telling me about children in a Buddhist refugee camp in southern Thailand that had the opportunity to hear the Gospel of Jesus Christ for the first time. (They were refugees of the tsunami of December 26, 2004.) I also received another report, this one from the Middle East, where school children in Bethlehem heard the Good News from a man who is taking one of our Kid's Evangelism Explosion training clinics there. Many of the children wanted to pray to receive Jesus. And I not only heard reports but also saw it with my own eyes when some EE-trained Christians headed up and led many desperate souls to Christ in New York after 9-11.

So, how does this light shine forth? Simple. Christians go. How can we say we are the light of God to the peoples of this nation and the world if we will not go to them?

Perhaps you are saying, "Great. I want to go but I don't know how." That is why we, at Evangelism Explosion, exist.[30] We will be happy to help you so that you can comfortably and confidently share Jesus with your friends, relatives, work associates, and neighbors. And, moreover, we will equip you to train others in your congregation how to witness as well. We have one-week Leadership Training clinics and launches at different churches. We also offer Share Your Faith workshops, where we will come out to your church and start by training some of your congregations in a one-day workshop. Feel free to contact our office for more information. Our job is to assist you to do the job that Jesus has called you to do.

After Hurricane Wilma in 2005, my family and I went 16 days without power in our home in Fort Lauderdale. During that time, I was scheduled to speak at a conference up in Baltimore the Tuesday a week after the storm (which had hit Monday). I did go to the conference, but I didn't feel comfortable leaving my wife and family without any way to cool the refrigerator or have a light in the evening. So I looked to buy a generator. I found one up in Orlando (about three hours north) and made the drive up Saturday morning. God showed me a vision that I hope I never forget.

While on the way back, I counted 52 power trucks driving down to South Florida. Some were from Georgia

---

[30] To contact us, please see http://www.eeinternational.org.

and North Carolina. Some were from Texas and Ohio. Some were even from Michigan and Canada! As I counted the trucks, a couple of thoughts hit me. This had to be really expensive to bring all these trucks down here. Think of the gas it would take to drive one of those huge trucks down all the way from Canada. And more than the money, think of the time that it would take for the men and women who left their homes and families to come and stay for several months working in South Florida. Why would they do it? Why would they go to all the expense? Then it hit me. They had one overriding belief that constrained their actions. This belief compelled them to go to whatever effort and cost necessary. This belief was this: that it is unacceptable for people to live in darkness, without power.

CONCLUSION

As Christians, we are the light of the world, and we must go and share this light. We should find it unacceptable for people to live in darkness, without the power of God. We are compelled by the Spirit of God to go. In fact, we can only truly be light when we go. Our truest and surest form of worshiping God is shown by our willingness to obey His command and to take His light to the ends of the earth. Let us carry His light and power to every people group on this planet. And the great news is that light always wins.

6

The Christian at Judgment

(Prepare for Eternity)

"Each one's work will become clear; for the Day will declare it, because it will be revealed by fire; and the fire will test each one's work, of what sort it is. If anyone's work which he has built on it endures, he will receive a reward."

1 Corinthians 3:13, 14

A certain gentleman died. And he was pumped, pimped, painted, laid out for all to see in the funeral parlor. And two of his friends came and stood before the bier and looked at the body. And then one of them said, dabbing a tear from her eye, "Well, old Harry has gone to his 'just reward.'" I am sure we have all heard that phrase at one time or another. Now if the dear lady meant by that what I think she meant by that, namely that "old Harry" had gone to Heaven, then that certainly is incorrect. Let's get it clear once and for all. Heaven is not anyone's just reward.

The Bible makes it abundantly clear that Heaven is a free gift, not an earned reward. In fact, the first question which Dr. Kennedy asked new members when they joined Coral Ridge Presbyterian Church makes this abundantly plain: "Do you acknowledge yourselves to be sinners in the sight of God, justly deserving His displeasure and without hope, save in His sovereign mercy?"

Yes, the truth is that Hell is the just reward of everyone. And Heaven is a free gift. We have seen that already. Heaven is given to those who trust in Christ. Dr. Kennedy told me one time of an experience he had that fits very nicely with this point. He said, "Some time ago, in Minneapolis, I was talking to some folks, and I said to them that I knew assuredly, beyond any shadow of a doubt that should I die, I would go immediately to Paradise. Now, realizing that they might have thought that that was some sort of spiritual braggadocio, some boasting on my part, I hastened to add that I also knew something else. I knew equally assuredly that I deserved to go to Hell. "In fact," I said, "I'll tell you something if you'll promise not to tell anyone else. I wouldn't want this to get around." They sort of leaned forward in their chairs a little bit. "The truth is they're my kind of people 'down there.'" They looked a little shocked. I said, "Furthermore, they're your kind of people down there too. The fact of the matter is, they are the only kind of people that there are. Sinners." Just like you and me.

I remember seeing a little pamphlet one time that had a provocative question on the cover. It said, "What must you do to go to Hell?" And I thought, "That's an interesting question. I'd be eager to see what the author has to say." So I opened it up. It was blank. That sort of gets the juices flowing. After a while I realized what he meant. What he meant was that there is nothing that you or I need to do in order to go to Hell because we have already done sufficient to get ourselves there. We have more than paid for our ticket already. We do not have to do a thing else besides. We are on our way in capital style.

I came across another tract with this question on the cover: "What must you do to go to Heaven?" I opened it. Again, the same content—it, too, was blank. The message obviously was that there is nothing we can do to go to Heaven because sufficient has already been done in this case as well.

However, we get to Heaven by what Christ has done. As Jesus said, "It is finished. Tetelastai. It is paid. It is done. It is enough."[31] As someone has well said, "It is not do—but done." That, my friends, is the Gospel in a nutshell. The Gospel of Christ is not do...do this and don't that and do the other. But done. Paid. Finished. Enough. Sufficient. Over. In full. By Christ. All we need do is by faith; simply trust in that which someone else has done.

Sometimes you hear people say, "Well, I believe that we have our Hell right here on earth." Have you heard that? Do you know something? These people are right in a sense.

---

[31] John 19:30.

77

The Bible teaches that we have a foretaste of our inheritance right here in this world. We get a little preview of coming attractions. And for those people who are on their way to you-know-where, they do get a foretaste of it in this life. However, that is just a foretaste. The Bible calls it an earnest of our inheritance. You know what earnest money is. When you put earnest money down on a piece of property what you are doing is simply this: you are promising more to come. And the Greek word, I think, is even more interesting. The Greek word for earnest is "arabone." And in Greek culture and society the word "arabone" meant "a swatch of material." If you were going to recover your couch, you would go down to the shop where they sold material, and you would look at all of the various rolls of material until you found one that you thought would fit the bill. Then, you would have them cut off a little piece of that fabric, and you would take that home and hold it up against the couch and the drapes and the wallpaper and the rug to see if it fit. And if it fit, then you would go back, and you would choose that fabric to recover the couch. Now nobody in their right mind would ever think of taking a swatch of material home and going through all of that trouble if they knew that that swatch was all that the shop had; was all that was available; that there was no more.

What God is telling us is yes, you may have a foretaste of Hell here in this life, but it is only the earnest. It is the "arabone." The whole roll is waiting for you when you die.

But that is bad news. And we are here really to proclaim Good News. And the Good News is that you can have a foretaste of Heaven. People say, "We have our Hell right here on earth." Well, you can have your Heaven right here on earth if that is where you're going. You have a foretaste of your inheritance. You will not have a foretaste of it now if you're not going to have the whole thing when you leave this world.

How many people, millions of people every week sing the song, "Blessed assurance, Jesus is mine. O what a foretaste of glory divine."[32] And they do not have the faintest notion of what they are singing, nor the slightest foretaste of what they are singing about.

Do you have a foretaste of "glory divine?" You can have a little bit of Heaven right here on earth. I hope that you do. If you do, you will have it by grace, not by just reward. The Scripture says, "It is by grace that we are saved" (based on Ephesians 2:8). Now there is an acrostic that I learned from Dr. Kennedy who heard it in Berlin at a great conference from the chaplain to the Queen of England. The chaplain said, "Grace, g-r-a-c-e stands for God's Riches At Christ's Expense." God's riches. Eternal life. In a new body, in a new world, in a new universe.

---

[32] Fanny J. Crosby, 1820 -1915.

Paradise. Enjoyed forevermore. At Christ's expense. The bloody sweat. The scourge. The spikes. The spear. The agony. The Hell that purchased the grace of God for us.

Heaven is a free gift. But you know heresies tend to come as twins. And if people do not succeed in falling into the embrace of the heresy which says that eternal life is something which they must earn by their own works and their own goodness, they will fall into the embrace of its twin. Namely, having received the gift of eternal life, now I can lie back in my hammock and do nothing. If Ephesians 2:8-9 says, *"For by grace you have been saved through faith, and that not of yourselves; it is the gift of God, not of works, lest anyone should boast."* Ephesians 2:10 says, *"For we are His workmanship, created in Christ Jesus for good works, which God prepared beforehand that we should walk in them."*

We are not saved by works. We are saved unto good works. It is not the cause. It is the effect. It is not the root. It is the fruit of salvation. Now somebody has already figured the whole thing out. What he is saying, they declare, is not that we are saved by simply faith alone or that we are saved by both. Wrong. False. Zero. Flunk. Missed it altogether. We are not saved by works, and we are not saved by faith plus works. We are saved by grace alone through faith alone. But we are saved for good works.

In this life, if you spend much time in school, you learn to take a lot of tests. We are a nation of test-takers, somebody said. Test taking has become in modern America, a major survival skill. What is incredibly sad is that few know about the most important test that any one of us is ever going to have to take, which is when we stand before the judgment of God.

We have seen that eternal life is a free gift. But let me say this: there are rewards in Heaven. There are degrees of reward in Heaven, even as there are degrees of punishment in Hell.

Concerning the latter, in Hell, the Bible talks about some receiving "the greater condemnation." For example, Jesus warned, *"...it will be more tolerable for Tyre and Sidon in the day of judgment than for you"* (Matthew 11:22-23).[33] After a parable warning us on being ready for His return, He noted, *"And that servant who knew his master's will, and did not prepare himself or do according to his will, shall be beaten with many stripes"* (Luke 12:47). There are degrees of punishment. And so there are various rewards in Heaven. The Bible speaks frequently about these rewards.

Notice, for example, Jesus said, *"Do not lay up for yourselves treasures on earth, where moth and rust destroy and where thieves break in and steal; but lay up for yourselves treasures in heaven"* (Matthew 6:19-20). Now that is not talking about salvation. That is talking about rewards that are given beyond salvation. *"Whatever you do,*

---

[33] In this passage Jesus was speaking of Chorazin and Bethsaida.

do it heartily, as to the Lord and not to men, knowing that from the Lord you will receive the reward" (Colossians 3:23-25). *"That You should reward Your servants the prophets and the saints"* (Revelation 11:18). And in Romans, it says that God *"...will render to each one according to his deeds"* (Romans 2:6). And in the last chapter of the Bible, Jesus Christ says, *"And behold, I am coming quickly and My reward is with Me"* (Revelation 22:12). And, of course, in 1 Corinthians 3:14, again, we read, *"If anyone's work which he has built on it endures, he will receive a reward."*

Let us consider then the matter of these rewards.

It is important to note that they are not "just rewards." Even our rewards are not based upon justice. Why? Because, note well, the best works of the best saints of God are imperfect and are tainted with sin; therefore, justly deserving of the condemnation of God. May I say that again? The best works of the best and greatest of saints are deserving of the disapproval, rejection, and condemnation of God. God cannot accept anything that is imperfect. God is of pure eyes that cannot look upon anything which is even tainted with sin, and our best works are all thus tainted. However, God having accepted our persons in Christ, and for the sake of Christ, is willing to receive our works, which are done in faith sincerely to His glory. He is willing to receive them and to overlook their imperfections and to graciously accept them for Christ's sake and even to graciously reward us for them.

But even the reward is of grace.

Now, let us consider what it is we do that will earn rewards. Well, for example, Christ told us, in an explicit promise of reward, *"Blessed are you when they revile and persecute you, and say all kinds of evil against you falsely for My sake. Rejoice and be exceedingly glad for great is your reward in heaven"* (Matthew 5:11-12). Now, may I point out to you that you will not be rewarded if you are persecuted and reviled because of your own orneriness. But that is not what this is talking about. It is only when you take upon yourself the name of Christ. When you bear witness to Him. When you identify yourself with His cause and you receive the opprobrium that the world holds for Christ. Then you will receive that persecution for His sake. And then you can rejoice and be exceedingly glad, for great is your reward in Heaven. And you take your stand with Him.

Concerning stewardship, Jesus said, *"...you were faithful over a few things, I will make you ruler over many things"* (Matthew 25:21). So God is willing to give rewards for faithful stewardship.

There are special rewards for loving enemies. The Bible says to love your enemies and do good. And lend, hoping for nothing again. And your rewards shall be great (based on Matthew 5:44, 42).

And most particularly, there are rewards for carrying out the Great Commission. Jesus said, *"Do you not say, 'There are still four months and then comes the harvest'? Behold, I say to you, lift up your eyes and look at the fields, for they are already white for harvest! And he who reaps receives wages, and gathers fruit for eternal life, that both he who sows and he who reaps may rejoice together"* (John 4:35-36). And the Bible says that, *"Those who are wise shall shine like the brightness of the firmament, and those who turn many to righteousness like the stars forever and ever"* (Daniel 12:3). Those who are faithful witnesses for Christ will receive abundant rewards.

I would ask you, what are you laying up in the way of treasures in Heaven? Many people assiduously work to lay up treasures in this life. They do exactly the opposite of what Jesus Christ said. They spend all of their lives laying up treasures in this earth, where moth and rust destroy while spending little time or effort in laying up treasures in Heaven.

1 Corinthians 3 says that Christ is the only foundation. *"As a wise master builder,"* said Paul, *"I have laid the foundation...which is Jesus Christ. [But] take heed,"* he says, *"how [you] build on it"* (1 Corinthians 3:10-11). We should take heed not only to the quantity of the work, but also to the quality of the work. There is a great deal of slovenly and slatternly work that goes on in the name of Christ. But it should be the very finest. There is a great

motto out in front of Coral Ridge Presbyterian Church on a marble slab that says, "Excellence in all things. And all things for God's glory." Unfortunately, many things are done in the name of Christ which are not done excellently.

Take heed how you build there upon. Some will build gold, silver, and precious stones. Others: wood, hay, and stubble.

Now the precious stones that are spoken of here, are not diamonds, rubies, sapphires, and emeralds. But rather, it is talking about building stones. We are talking about building a building to God. We are talking about marble and granite and other such fine stone as that. It says that some people are just building out of wood, hay, and stubble. And in that great day—the day of the Great Assize, the Final Judgment—in that day, the fire will try our works, of what sort they are. And the gold, silver, and precious stones will remain. But the wood, hay, and stubble will go up in an instantaneous conflagration. The fire will try it, and it will be reduced to white ash at our feet.

The most calamitous tragedy that could ever possibly befall a human being is described in the simple words of the Gospel where it talks about the fact of people losing their own souls. The implications of that term are so momentous that they stagger the mind. To lose you own soul. To come to the judgment as an unbeliever and to hear the solemn pronouncement of doom by the Great Judge. *"I never knew you; depart from Me, you who practice lawlessness!"* (Matthew 7:23). To be bound hand and foot and to be cast into outer darkness where there is weeping and wailing and gnashing of teeth. That is the greatest disaster that could ever befall a human being. But the second worse disaster is to have all the work of your life burnt up.

Suppose tonight, in your sleep, there were an unexpected fire in your home, and your home burnt to the ground, with your car or cars in the garage exploding in the fire. Everything you have. You rush out the door with nothing but your pajamas. All of your possessions are in there. Let's say that you have also lost your job. You have no savings. You have nothing but the pajamas on your back. Even your family is gone. You're turned out into the street. A whole lifetime of work is gone in a night.

Consider the anguish, grief, and agony of heart and mind. To lose a whole lifetime of work. That is what some of you will experience, only infinitely worse at the Judgment. *"If anyone's work is burned, he will suffer loss; but he himself will be saved, yet so as through fire"* (1 Corinthians 3:15). He will not have any rewards. The results of his lifetime will have produced nothing.

Now, what exactly, is the nature of these rewards? The Bible never describes them. But we may know that they are of inestimable value. And the Bible says that we should earnestly seek them and work toward them. I do not know what they are. But I know that we will suffer the loss of them if we are not faithful.

Is your life being lived for something that counts? I would ask you this: in the past week, what did you do that will have any meaning at all a million years from now? The majority of you, if you were honest, would say nothing.

Matthew Arnold may have described your life in poetry:

> What is the course of the life
>
> Of mortal men on the earth?
>
> Most men eddy about
>
> Here and there—eat and drink,
>
> Chatter and love and hate,
>
> Gather and squander, are raised
>
> Aloft, and hurled into the dust,
>
> Striving blindly, achieving
>
> Nothing; and then they die
>
> Perish—and no one asks
>
> Who or what they have been
>
> More than he asks what waves
>
> In the moonlit solitudes mild
>
> Of the midmost ocean have swelled
>
> Foam'd for a moment, and disappeared.

Was that your life in poetry? Wood, hay, and stubble or gold, silver, and precious stones? Are you living your life for Christ and His Kingdom? Building on that which is eternal?

You know, you often hear the statement that the Church is full of hypocrites. Now of course, there is a great element of truth in that. There are many hypocrites in the Church. But something that you never hear is that there are saints in the Church. And some of you, at the judgment, are going to receive a great shock. And I want to forewarn you about it right now. On the one hand, you are going to discover that there are people in the Church of Christ (universal), who are so incredibly faithful to Christ, who year after year and month after month and week after week, live their lives for the service of Christ. They are concerned for things that are eternal; they are building the Kingdom of Jesus Christ and living for His glory. They work and give of themselves to His cause. On the other hand, at the judgment, you are going to be astounded. Why you thought everybody was like you, who did nothing. It is sadly true that 20% of the people in the church do 80% of the work. And if you're part of that 80% that do 20% of the work and many who do none of it, you probably did not even know that such faithful, diligent people existed. Well, in that day, you will know. And you will be saddened by the fact that you were not to be found among them. They shall suffer loss—an inestimable and eternal and unalterable loss. Well has it been said: Only one life and soon 'tis passed. And only what's done for Christ will last. May I write that on the walls of your heart? Only, only one life and soon 'tis passed. And only what is done for Christ shall last.

CONCLUSION

I pray that God would stir us up by His Spirit and cause us to be faithful and diligent, to be good laborers in His vineyard. I ask that He would strengthen us to seek those things which are above and to labor for those things which are eternal, and that we would do all this to the glory of Christ and the advancement of His Kingdom.

KNOW

Part II

7

God's Purpose For Our Lives

(Know Your Purpose)

"Go therefore and make disciples of all the nations, baptizing them in the name of the Father and of the Son and of the Holy Spirit, teaching them to observe all things that I have commanded you; and lo, I am with you always, even to the end of the age." Amen.

Matthew 28:19, 20

"Then God blessed them, and God said to them, 'Be fruitful and multiply; fill the earth and subdue it; have dominion over the fish of the sea, over the birds of the air, and over every living thing that moves on the earth.'"

Genesis 1:28

I have a question for you—a very, very important question: What are you living for? What is the purpose of your life?

Socrates said that an unexamined life is not worth living, but I am afraid that the situation is more serious than that. An unexamined life might bring us into disastrous conflict with God who calls us to examine ourselves. What is your purpose for living?

The famed preacher, Dr. Louis Evans of the Great Hollywood Presbyterian Church, years ago was invited to a

93

frat house at UCLA where a large number of young men were there to hear him speak. Some were sitting on couches, others filled every chair, some were on the floor, and some were just leaning against the wall. For his opening statement, he said, "Gentlemen, what is your purpose for living?"

One of them raised their hand and said, "Well, I'm studying business. I plan to go on and get an M.B.A. and want to have a successful business one day."

He said, "That's very commendable. However, that is how you are going to make your living. What are you living for?"

"Oh."

Another raised his hand and said, "Well, you see, pastor, I'm looking for the girl of my dreams, and when I find her I'm going to get married and we're going to have six kids, because I love kids and I'm going to live for my family."

He said, "That's wonderful. Those are the people you are going to be living with, but what are you living for?

Another said, "I want a big beautiful home in the suburbs with a swimming pool and all of the modern conveniences."

And he said, "Well, that's nice, but that's where you are going to be living, but what are you living for?" Now I have a feeling that Dr. Evans just shot down some of your reasons for living as well as those fraternity students. What are you living for? What is the purpose, really, of your life?

Now purpose is very important. There are eight different Greek words in the New Testament that are translated purpose. Sixty-two times it occurs. Purpose. God acts by purpose. He is fulfilling His purpose. The angels of God act according to His purpose. We are senescent and rational creatures. We live by purpose, where animals live by instinct. We have reason and purpose. Everything we do we do on purpose, and when you ask somebody, "Why did you do that," and they say, "I don't know," they are pulling your leg, because we all do whatever we do on purpose.

Now some of those purposes may be low and mean and base, or they may be high and exalted, but we do everything we do by purpose. But most of us do not ever examine our purposes very carefully.

Those that founded this country, however, had and did, and left for us a very clear record of what their purpose was. I would like for you to hear it because I think they had it exactly right. When all of the New England colonies had been established over here, they got together for the first time in 1643 and wrote what is known as the New England Confederation. In that they stated these words—listen to them carefully: "Whereas we all came into these parts of America with one and the same end and aim, namely, to advance the Kingdom of our Lord Jesus Christ and to enjoy the liberties of the Gospel in purity with peace..." [34]

I guarantee you that you will rarely, if ever, hear that in any public school in this country today, but that is why they came. Now notice something. They were farmers, builders, blacksmiths, teachers, doctors, and many other things. They had many ancillary purposes, but one overriding main purpose toward which all of the other purposes were merely tributary, and that was that no matter what they did, they were doing all they could to advance the kingdom of our Lord Jesus Christ. Can you say: We all came into this part of America for one and the same end and aim—to advance the kingdom of our Lord Jesus Christ? Is that why you are here? I want you to know something. That is why I am here. That is why I came to Fort Lauderdale. I hope it is why you are here on earth. I would like for you to see how important that is.

But no matter what other minor purposes we have, we have to have a central purpose. By the way, all of those Founders, I would like to tell those frat students, made a living. All of them reared families—well, most all of them. And all of them built houses and lived in them, but those were not the reasons for their living. That was not their purpose. They were living to advance the kingdom of Jesus Christ. Purpose. Something given to us by God, who is the

---

[34]The New England Confederation, in *The Annals of America* (Chicago, et al.: Encyclopedia Britannica, 1976), Volume 1, 172.

God that is working out everything for His own purposes in this world.

Now, if you were ever at a garbage dump with seeing eyes, you would discover something: that the things which are there are things that no longer fulfill their purpose—the purpose for which they were made or the purpose for which you bought them. Having ceased to fulfill that purpose, they are thrown into the garbage. A plate broken no longer serves the purpose of holding food and is thrown away. Take, for example, the bone of a T-bone steak. You bought it to provide a meal. It did. Now it no longer serves the purpose (at least what's left of it), and you throw it away, along with grapefruit rinds and egg shells and a whole lot of other stuff—bread that got stale and a thousand other things that no longer serve the purpose for which they were made or for which you bought them.

When pagans lived in Jerusalem before David conquered it, there was a valley (called the Valley of Hinnom) outside the wall of Jerusalem that was used for one of the pagan gods. There was a great metal image of the god situated there. It was hollow, and they would build huge fires inside of it until the image glowed red hot. After the statue was turned into blazing metal, they would place in the extended hands their babies as an offering and sacrifice to this bloodthirsty god.

When the people of God conquered that city, they destroyed the altar and metal image by covering it with their garbage. They set it on fire and continued thereafter to put all of their garbage on top of it until it became the garbage dump of Jerusalem. It was always burning, always consuming the garbage. And what was in the garbage? Things that no longer fulfilled their purpose.

Jesus used the Valley of Hinnom, which in Hebrew reads "Gehenna". "Gehenna" is one of the words in the Bible that means "Hell." What is Hell? It is a place where things are cast into which do not fulfill the purpose for which they were created. Think about that. Do you belong there? Where the worm dies not and the fire is not quenched—"Gehenna"—the garbage dump of the universe.

What is the purpose that God has given us? A person said to Dr. Kennedy one time: "I just don't know what my purpose in life should be. I haven't chosen a purpose yet." He answered them, "Wonderful. I am glad to hear it, because you should not." You see, we have been sold the humanistic bill of goods that says that we are autonomous. Now the word autonomous comes from two Greek words: "autos", which means self, and "nomos", which means law. The autonomous man is a law unto himself. He would be "god," and he will have whatever purpose he decides to have. "I did it my way." And that has overspread this nation like sticky glue, and many, many people have bought into it.

We are not gods; we are not autonomous. We are creatures made in the image of the almighty God, and we have been created for His purpose. Not yours and not mine. I hope that you get a good hold on that because it can certainly change your life. Our nation's settlers had it right. What they wrote really is astonishing, and it's a shame you will rarely hear it in our schools. They, from all of the colonies, came together to advance the kingdom of our Lord Jesus Christ. There is your purpose.

Now how do we do that? It is spelled out in the first and last commands that God has given: the Alpha and the Omega, the beginning and the end of God's mandates for the human race—the first one given in Genesis 1:28. The first mentions that God created us in His image, that we should subdue the earth and have dominion over all things in it. As the vice-regents of God, we are in His place to bring to pass His will in all of the various spheres of life.

And so, the Founders of America went about fulfilling what is known as the Cultural Mandate by establishing Godly and righteous institutions, whether they were schools or colleges or governments or whatever. They were established according to the righteous principles of God. For example, when the Founding Fathers wrote up the template for all future states to be added to the United States of America, note what they said about the priorities of education: "Religion, morality, and knowledge being necessary to good government and the happiness of mankind, schools and the means of education shall forever be encouraged."[35] These words were adopted in 1787 and re-adopted in 1789 by the same men who gave us the first amendment (which today is misinterpreted to mean that there should be a strict separation of church and state—by which the secularists really mean, a separation of God and state).

We are told to go and make disciples of all nations teaching them to *"observe all things that I have commanded you"* (Matthew 28:20). And so, alas, we have withdrawn from that today and have for almost a hundred years. The result is that into that vacuum left by Christians, unbelievers have flocked, and we have godless schools, godless colleges, godless governments (as much as they have been able to), godless entertainment, and godless everything.

I have heard it said that virtually every newspaper in 1850 in America was owned and operated by Christians who gave published sermons every Sunday in their paper with a leading theologian who gave commentary with Scripture quotations in them and argued from Christian principles. Can you name one daily newspaper today run by Christians? I cannot. There may be some, but I do not know of them. We have left the field of battle, and so the unbelievers have come.

---

[35] The Northwest Ordinance, Article III, in ibid., Volume 3, 194-195.

We sing "This Is My Father's World"[36] or "To God Be the Glory,"[37] and yet we have turned everything of this world over to Satan. Look at what is taught in our schools, what is found in our libraries, what is found on our computers on the web, what is found in our theaters and television. It is the devil that gets the glory for this world, all too often I am afraid.

The last commandment that Christ gave right before being taken up to Heaven was that we were to go and make disciples to all nations. "You shall be my witnesses." It is repeated four times in four slightly different ways, but it is clearly stated that we are to take the Gospel of Jesus Christ to a lost and needy world. That is something that so desperately needs to be done, and I thank God that there are so many Christians that are eagerly and joyfully doing it. However, I know that there are many professing Christians that do not.

The Church is in some ways like a college. In a college there are two kinds of courses. There are required courses and there are electives. Now you can take all of the electives that you would like to take, depending upon your talents and interests and the time that you have available. But there are some required courses that you must take if you have any hopes of graduating. Imagine a student two

---

[36] Words by Maltbie D. Babcock, 1901. Arranged by Franklin L. Sheppard in his *Alleluia*, 1915.

[37] Words by Fanny Crosby, in *Brightest and Best*, by W. H. Doane and Robert Lowry (Chicago, Illinois: Biglow & Main, 1875), number 118. Arranged by W. Howard Doane.

weeks before graduation, after having spent four years in college, coming to the dean and saying, "I've been reading over the catalog. I noticed you have all of these 'required' courses. I declared my major in engineering, and this says something about needing to take a bunch of mathematics courses. Well, I didn't take any mathematics…I took basket weaving, Chinese art, modern dance, and rock and roll in the sixties. I never got around to this math, and then there's the matter of all these science courses…I mean, really? But Dean, I want you to know that getting this engineering degree is really, really important to me because I've told everyone that I'm going to be an engineer. I understand that is a very lucrative profession, so I want that certificate. I will get it, won't I?"

Should we take a vote on that? Is there anybody who would suppose that the college was going to grant that student an engineering degree? And how would you like to drive across the bridge that he designed? Of course, he's not going to get the degree.

We are to be salt and light. Salt in that we keep the culture from utterly corrupting; light in that we bring into the darkness of men's mind the light of the glorious Gospel of Christ. We are told to seek first the kingdom of God. How do we do that? By fulfilling the Cultural Mandate and the Great Commission. That is exactly how the Founding Fathers did it. We pray, "Your will be done on earth as it is in Heaven." We are to build the kingdom of Jesus Christ here on earth while we are here, as we are in Heaven forever.

It is amazing how many people do not take a long look at life. Dr. Kennedy used to tell a story about a boy named "Little Johnnie," and it went something like this: "Little Johnnie was twelve years old, and he lived right near the ocean. And his great joy was to play on the beach and the water in the summer. One Saturday morning he decided to build the greatest castle in the sand that had ever been built, and he brought all of the pails and buckets and shovels of every size, and all of the various other implements that he might need and accoutrements. And he had little soldiers and little cannons to put over the moats on the wall, and he began to work on his plan. There was a marvelous moat and there were Babylon-like walls. There were tall towers, turrets, spires, and even little flags on the top. He worked for five or six hours without even thinking about lunch or the fact that the sun was westering. And since he was facing the castle, he did not notice that the tide was coming in until the waves got bigger and closer, and at length one particularly large one crashed right behind his ankles over the moat, leveling the walls and turning his castles and spires into a big puddle of sand. He stood with water and sand dripping from his hands, looking at his life's work, almost, in utter dismay. We say, 'What a foolish child. I mean, didn't he know the tides came in and out? Is he that stupid?'

"Well, before we too harshly condemn him, we are adults, for the most part here. Do we not know that the tide is coming in? Do we not know that the crashing wave of God's judgment is soon going to come upon every one of us? Have you been building on nothing but sand? A thousand years from now, what will what you have done in this life amount to—a million years, a hundred years?" For most people it would be nothing. You have wasted your life because you have had your own autonomous purposes, and you have not yielded yourself to the purpose of God for your life. But remember, that's what the garbage heap is for.

When we realize that we have failed to do what God put us on this earth to do, we realize the results of that. Not only has the magnificent patrimony that has been given to us by the Founders—a Godly Christian nation—been allowed to slip through our fingers like sand and become this Godless monstrosity that we see around us today, but more than that, innumerable millions of souls in America have and are and will perish eternally in "Gehenna" because the Church has failed to heed the purpose for which it was created.

What do we do? My friend, the answer is very simple. The word is singular. It is simply this. Repent! That's the first thing that Jesus said when he began His ministry. Repent. He had all of eternity to think about what he would say to the human race when He finally got here, and He came into Galilee preaching the Gospel of the kingdom of God and saying, *"The time is fulfilled, and the kingdom of God is at hand. Repent, and believe in the gospel"* (Mark 1:15). The Great Commission is not an elective, and without the core course, no one graduates from God's college. To willfully disobey the commander-in-chief is rank insubordination and results inevitably in a court marshal. On a ship it is mutiny. There was a time when you would have walked the plank. That was their garbage heap, the ocean.

What is your purpose for life? We are to be witnesses to Jesus Christ. Everything is to be brought into that great purpose. Also, we are to use whatever gifts and talents God has given us for His honor and glory.

Look at some great examples throughout history.

God had gifted Johann Sebastian Bach with great musical talent. He wrote every note to the glory of Jesus Christ. His music is still performed, in and out of the Church. He witnesses to the glory of Jesus Christ, even centuries after his death.

One of the great orators of all time was William Wilberforce, a member of Parliament in the last half of the 18th century. When he converted to Jesus Christ, he had already been in politics, but was considering getting out in order to pursue the ministry. Thankfully, John ("Amazing Grace") Newton, a former slave trader who had become a pastor, encouraged Wilberforce to use his politics as his ministry. The latter did and accomplished wonderful things for the glory of God, including the abolition of the slave trade in the British Empire and the freeing of all slaves therein.

God gave C. S. Lewis great literary talents. Suppose he had abandoned his calling as a writer and as a professor of literature (at Oxford and then Cambridge), and instead, he hobbled together whatever support he could to go into the mission field. The world would be much poorer. Almost fifty years after his death, his witness to Jesus Christ continues. But note: that is through his books, not just his personal evangelism.

In short, use whatever talents and whatever opportunities God has given you for His honor and glory and for the spreading of His glorious Gospel. When a life is unexamined and the purposes that God had for making us in the first place are ignored, denied, and refused, there can only be one outcome.

CONCLUSION

If God's commands are obeyed, the results can be glorious, and this nation could be revived. We could see righteousness again prevail in America as millions of people come to know the wonder of the Savior and their lives are changed. Can you imagine how different this country would be if suddenly those Founders who met together in New England to sign that Confederation were suddenly multiplied into two hundred and some million people, and they all could say, "We have come into these parts of America for one and the same end and aim, to advance the kingdom of our Lord Jesus Christ." May it be. May it be.

8

The Single-Minded, Sold-Out Servant

(Know Your Place)

"...the kingdom of heaven is like treasure hidden in a field, which a man found..."

Matthew 13:44

We had just entered Kosovo and were driving through a mountain pass that lies between Macedonia and Kosovo. The road was very rough because of the bombs that had been dropped during the Kosovo war. We got tired of the rough roads and stopped for a break. Tom Stebbins started off into the grass next to the road. The night before I had heard a story on the BBC about land mines in Kosovo. At the last moment before Tom stepped into the grass I shouted, "STOP!" Moments later a Jeep came around the corner, and men jumped out and told us that the area was filled with land mines. Three days later, as we left via the same road, we saw all the flags that were placed by the bombs, and there were five land mines directly in the area

Tom was about to walk into. Aren't you glad we do not have to deal with land mines everyday?

However, we all live in a world of land mines. There is danger everywhere around us. The Bible talks of one land mine far more real than the hunks of metal and plastic explosives that we faced in Kosovo. What is this land mine? How can we recognize it?

Look around you. Note your wallet, your car, your house, your bank account, and your retirement savings. Watch out—they are land mines.

The Bible tells us that this land mine is materialism— the love of stuff. This is a big issue to God. In Matthew 6:24, we learn that you cannot serve both God and money. In the Ten Commandments, God demands that we *"have no other gods before [Him]"* (Exodus 20:3). In Matthew 13, Jesus explains the parable of the sower. He tells us that the cares of this world and the deceitfulness of riches choke the word. So you can see, the love of this world's goods is a very real danger to our lives both here and eternally.

Let us look at a parable in Matthew that brings God's view of material things into sharper focus.

Matthew 13:44: *"Again, the kingdom of heaven is like treasure hidden in a field, which a man found and hid; and for joy over it he goes and sells all that he has and buys that field."*

A few notes of explanation in interpreting this parable:

First of all, this is not a standard parable. Earlier, in verses 34-35, Jesus said His purpose of parables was to keep the things of God secret. In verse 13, Jesus says, *"Therefore I speak to them in parables, because seeing they do not see, and hearing they do not hear, nor do they understand. And in them the prophecy of Isaiah is fulfilled, which says: 'Hearing you will hear and shall not understand, and seeing you will see and not perceive.'"* However, in this case (because He is intending to explain things to His disciples), He is not trying to hide anything.

Secondly, when you see the word "like" it refers to the whole parable. So this is not saying the Kingdom of Heaven is like a man. It is not saying the Kingdom of Heaven is like a man discovering a treasure. It is saying that the Kingdom of Heaven is like the whole story in the parable.

Last, when we interpret parables, it is good to concentrate on the one main thing that the parable is about. As I studied this parable, many commentators try to make each part of the parable mean some long and varied things. "The grass in the field is the Bible, the man searching was reading the Bible... etc." Let's resist that. Let's look for the one simple truth that God the Spirit has placed here for us.

In this parable we learn of a man who was walking along in a field one day when, wonder of wonders, he discovered a treasure. This treasure was buried in a field. Perhaps he had a walking stick, and the stick went through the soil. Perhaps he was digging in the field. Maybe he rented the field. Maybe he worked there. Regardless, he discovered this treasure, and it changed his focus for that day. It changed his focus for life. I do not know what his plans for that day were (I am sure he had some), but they were dropped. He determined that he would get that treasure no matter what it cost. He truly became single-minded.

SINGLE-MINDED THOUGHTS

So we come to the first help in avoiding the land mine of materialism in our lives: be single-minded in your thinking.

The treasure in this parable is the Kingdom of Heaven, which implies eternal life and our relationship to Christ. For you to be single-minded about the desire for this treasure, you must first understand its value. Had this man not understood the value of this treasure, his response would have been very different. How about you? Have you discovered the treasure of the Kingdom of Heaven; of eternal life; of a relationship with Christ? Have you truly understood its value?

When I first started at Evangelism Explosion, I was astonished at how few pastors that I met were really interested in evangelism (telling people about eternal life). EE had so changed my life that I could not imagine why everyone would not be involved. But the reality is, only a small percentage of pastors that I knew were involved in

EE (or any evangelism equipping ministry). One day, I asked Dr. Kennedy why he thought this was the case. He said, "I don't think they believe in Heaven and Hell. They are not really convinced that they're real. If God would dip all pastors into Hell for a fraction of a second and then pull them out with the soles of their shoes melting off, charred with soot, I believe their commitment to the Great Commission would substantially increase." I agree. It is critical that we see that the treasure is real and that we see it before it is too late.

You remember the story of the rich man and Lazarus? The day that both died, Lazarus was in the bosom of Abraham, while the rich man was tormented in Hell. What was the rich man's reaction once he became convinced of the reality of Heaven and Hell? He said, *"I beg you therefore, father, that you would send [Lazarus] to my father's house, for I have five brothers, that he may testify to them, lest they also come to this place of torment"* (Luke 16:27-28). You see, once you're convinced it is real; you're going to want to tell others, especially family, about it.

Second, you have to value it more than the things you have.

We have such an addiction to the things we own. Our possessions really are land mines waiting to destroy us. A perfect example was the rich, young ruler who asked Jesus what he must do to inherit eternal life (get the treasure). Jesus told him to sell all he had and give it to the poor and come and follow him. What did he do? He went away sad. Why? Because he had great wealth and didn't want to give it up.

We have to avoid the land mine of materialism and be single-minded about this treasure.

But it wasn't just the man's thinking that was changed. It was his actions as well.

SOLD OUT ACTIONS

So our second help in avoiding the land mine of materialism in our lives is to be sold-out in our actions.

It is one thing to say something; it is another to do what you say. Talk is cheap. If you're single-minded in your thinking, you will be sold-out in your actions. He was not only willing to, but did, give up everything he had for this treasure. And, he did it with joy.

He gave up everything.

He gained everything.

Jim Elliott said, "He is no fool who gives up what he can not keep to gain what he can not lose."[38]

David Livingstone, the Scottish physician and missionary to Africa, is said to be the first white man into the deepest interior of Africa. I have visited both of his graves. I remember when I stood by his grave in Westminster Abbey in London and another that is said to

---

[38] Elisabeth Elliot, *Through Gates of Splendor* (Carol Stream, IL: Tyndale House, 1957).

be the home of his heart in Victoria Falls, Zimbabwe. Here was a man who literally gave up everything to serve God. He was gone for five years at a time. He lost a child while he was away. He lost his wife to sickness when she came to visit him. He is said to have buried her and then fallen on the mound of dirt to weep. He then got up and sat under a tree and wrote an entry in his diary. What did he write? Did he complain to God over the hardship of his life? No. He wrote: "My Lord, My God, My King, My Savior, My all-in-all. This day I consecrate myself once more to you and pledge to value nothing save Your kingdom."

Livingstone and the man in this parable are two examples of men who avoided the land mine of materialism and were sold-out in their actions. They valued nothing except the treasure.

SATISFACTION

Now, our last help in avoiding the land mine of materialism in our lives: be satisfied.

Someone said that the true meaning of contentment is wanting what you have. If your heart's desire is eternal life and a relationship with Christ, you will not constantly be searching for material things.

The man in the parable gained the goal of his life. He was not a man to pity. He was filled with joy. He was rich beyond belief. He was satisfied.

Are we giving up our lives to serve God? If so, I think it is unwise for us to consider what we are doing as sacrifice. It is important to note that this man did what he did out of self-interest. We are not instructed to give up everything with no gain. In Matthew 6:44, Jesus tells us to lay up for ourselves treasures in Heaven. He does not tell us not to invest for gain, but just to invest in what is smart and to avoid investing in what is stupid. We will focus on this even more in a later chapter.

Are you single-minded in your thinking? Are you sold-out in your actions? Are you satisfied with your prize? I started out talking about the land mine of materialism. I have contrasted that with the Kingdom of Heaven. And here's why. I believe that at some point God will make us choose between our stuff and the Kingdom of Heaven. Perhaps many times in our lives this will happen. History is full of people who chose this world and fell on the land mines. But there are also examples of those who, like the man in this parable, chose the true treasure.

Abraham is a good example of someone who God caused to choose. For a better inheritance, he left his native land and all of its wealth. He chose to live in tents on the fringes of the Promised Land. When God promised to give him a son, Abraham waited for a long time (about twenty-five years). Finally, Isaac was born against all odds. I think you could see how Abraham would quickly fall in love with this child. If you think about it, you can almost see him take the tiny baby in his awkward arms. You can see him watching the boy grow. You can see him becoming all the things God had promised. Do you think there was anything more valuable to Abraham? But then God said, *"Take now your son."* (Genesis 22:2).

I doubt that there was a more agonizing evening spent by a man on earth, save Gethsemane, than the night before Abraham took the boy to kill him. God let him go through with it up until the point of no return, and then He stopped him. Abraham had given up everything. He was a man wholly surrendered, a man of utter obedience, a man whose possessions had no hold on him.

Now, it is not that he did not have anything. Had you asked Abraham's neighbors, they might have told you that Abraham was a very rich guy. But what if you had asked Abraham? He had a lot, but he possessed nothing.

So here's the big deal...which will you choose? Jesus said, *"...whoever desires to save his life will lose it, but whoever loses his life for My sake will find it."* (Matthew 16:25).

Abraham avoided the land mine of materialism.

CONCLUSION

A.W. Tozer once said, "If we would indeed know God in growing intimacy, we must go the way of renunciation."[39]

---

[39] A.W. Tozer, *The Pursuit of God* (Camp Hill, PA: Christian Publications, 1993), 30.

And if we are set upon the pursuit of God, He will sooner or later bring us to this test. Abraham's testing was, at the time, not known to him as such, yet if he had taken some course other than the one he did, the whole history of the Old Testament would have been different. God would have found his man, no doubt, but the loss to Abraham would have been tragic beyond the telling. So, we will be brought one by one to the testing place, and we may never know when we are there. At that testing place, there will be no dozen possible choices for us—just one and an alternative —but our whole future will be conditioned by the choice we make. May God grant us the grace to treasure that which really matters and not to be distracted by the baubles of this world.

9

The Church in the 21st Century

(Know Your Church)

"Who is she who looks forth as the morning, fair as the moon, clear as the sun, awesome as an army with banners?"

Song of Solomon 6:10

As we continue to consider God's guidance in our lives and what He would have us do, we want to step back and take a look at what He is doing right now at this present time in the world. Despite all the bad news that seems to hit us regularly, the worldwide picture of the Kingdom of God is actually quite encouraging. Much of this is behind the scenes. It is quite evident that "Aslan" is on the move![40]

---

[40] Aslan, the "Great Lion", is the central character in *The Chronicles of Narnia*. The author, C. S. Lewis, described Aslan as an alternative version of Christ—that is, as the form in which Christ might have appeared in a fantasy world.

We begin our look by considering a largely neglected book of the Old Testament.

THE SONG OF SOLOMON

The Song of Solomon is a marvelous book. It is beauteous, poignant, tender, and touching—the story of a love affair. On the surface, it is the story of a love affair of a man and a woman—of Solomon and the Shulammite woman. And yet, those who know the Scripture know there is a higher meaning as well, though there are many great lessons in that aspect of it. But it is also, ultimately, the story of the relationship of the Heavenly Bridegroom and His earthly bride—the Church.

It is an astounding book in many ways because we see much blessing and praising on either side. The Church praises and blesses her Lord, and the Lord praises and blesses the Church. He says He cannot see how He could live without us. He goes to and fro throughout the earth looking into the hearts of believers to find that which is excellent, to find that which is spiritual, to find that which is sincere Christianity, to find that love—that true love of Him. When He finds it, He does not hesitate to praise it unstintingly. I guarantee you that a study of this book will make you realize, perhaps more than ever before, how much you are loved by Christ. Hopefully that will result in a greater love on your part for Him.

How marvelous is His praise. That praise is found in our text: *"Who is she that looks forth as the morning, fair as the moon, clear as the sun, awesome as an army with banners?"* (Song of Solomon 6:10). That, I think, is one of the most, if not the most, glorious pictures the Church (you and me) to be found anywhere in the Scripture.

Note what it says: *"Who is she...?"* We are the bride of Christ. *"Who is she that looks forth as the morning?"* In the midst of the blackness of night of hopelessness, despair, and death, it is the Church that brings the hope of the sun rising. The Church even in the most ancient of days was the morning star that gave some hope of the coming morning to those who were lost in that darkness.

Even in the Old Testament, when darkness still covered most of the earth, she was that fair moon that gave, though borrowed, light to a needy and hopeless world—a world that could see nothing beyond that hole in the ground where life had little meaning and no hope. There was the Church, even back then, that was fair as the moon. That is, of course, an idealized picture of the Church. Unfortunately, there are many who would be seen merely as pockmarks on that moon. Nevertheless that is the picture He draws of the Church.

WHEN CHRIST AROSE

And yet there came a glorious day when the night was to fade away, and in that bright and marvelous morning when

Jesus Christ walked out of the tomb and the darkness of death faded away forever, the Church became clear as the sun and cast its light into the darkness and into the sadness and weeping of the bereaved who stood beside the tombs of their lost loved ones. It cast its light even into the midst of the idolatrous temple of the heathen and brought into that darkness the wonderful light of Christ, the true God and Savior. The light it cast illumined the hovel and the palace. That light spread, first from Jerusalem and then all around the world. That light brought about the establishment of this nation. That light has pierced every continent, gone into the deepest jungles, brought light to the darkness and to the most benighted heathen, the cannibals and headhunters in the depths of New Guinea. That light has taken away that fear of death, that bondage to sin. That light has set men free. That light continues to spread across the widest oceans and through the densest jungles and over the widest deserts to bring the light of Christ to men everywhere.

Just through the ministry of Evangelism Explosion alone, millions of people are being touched in our world today by that light of Jesus Christ.

The Church is to be *"...awesome as an army with banners"* (v. 10b). As that light has covered the whole world, the Church is seen again in this final revelation as an army. And we are that army of Christ. We sing, "Onward

Christian soldiers, marching as to war."[41] We are Christian soldiers in the army of Christ. He is the Captain of the well-fought fight that goes on before us. We are called to a great battle with the forces of darkness, with principalities and powers of the air.

It is interesting to note that the great Church statistician, David Barrett, has pointed out that at any given point in Christian history—in the beginning, in the middle, and even now—about one in every two hundred Christians has been martyred for his or her faith. He said the reason that anti-Christian persecution seems to be accelerating in our time (in the remnant Communist countries and in the Muslim countries) is a result of the growth of the Church. Persecution is part and parcel of the spread of the Christian Gospel. It is the enemy of our souls fighting back. As the book of Revelation notes, the devil is full of fury for he knows his time is short.[42]

We are called to go forth *"awesome as an army with banners."* We have a banner, Isaiah says. It is the Gospel. The Church has many banners. "Jesus Christ is Lord" was one of the earliest Ones. "He will never leave us" is another. "He always leads us forth in victory" is yet another. "He is King of kings and Lord of lords," is yet

---

[41] Words by Sabine Baring-Gould, *Church Times* (1865). Arranged by Arthur S. Sullivan (1871).

[42] Revelation 12:12.

another. "He goes forth upon a white horse conquering and to conquer" is yet another of the banners of Christ.

As it is with the armies of this world, when we see the flag, our national emblem, lifted up, even soldiers who are fatigued will renew their strength. So we, as the army of Christ are to go forth in that way. We should strike fear into those who are the enemies of God and the enemies of righteousness and godliness. I believe that we have seen the Church do just that down through the centuries—from a thousand years before Christ, when this Song of Solomon was first penned, down to that glorious resurrection morning after the passion at Calvary, down through the centuries of church history, on until today. And we should look forward to the Church as the 21st century unfolds. What will that be like? I am not a prophet, nor the son of a prophet.

One theologian has said that the future turns on so many tiny ball bearings that no one can prophesy it accurately who is not divinely inspired to do so. Yet, I believe there are some trends which, we trust, if they continue, will indeed result in the 21st century having a Church the like of which has not been seen before.

Through the depths of the Dark Ages the Gospel was almost hidden. Then, in the 1500s, through Martin Luther, John Calvin, John Knox, and others, the Gospel was brought to light again, and a glorious spiritual transformation took place. It grew somewhat slowly until

200 years ago when the modern missionary movement began. Then the Gospel for the first time went out from Europe into the East and the West until it traveled all around the world. The 19th century was the century of world missions, which took the Gospel everywhere. We have seen the enormous conquests that have been made by that missionary movement.

Tremendous change has taken place over the past century as a result of the Gospel traveling around the world.

In 1900, Christians (of all varieties) in the Third-World countries numbered about 87 million (15.6%), while Western countries reported over 470 million (84.4%).

By 1980, that figure had radically changed to 631.8 million (out of 1.433 billion Christians) in the Third-World (44.1%). The Western world slipped to 546.6 million (38.2%), while the Communist world grew to 254.1 million (17.7%). By that point, nearly half of the world's Christians now lived in the Third-World.

By the year 2000, 983.9 millions Christians (out of 2.01 billion) lived in the Third-World (48.7%) while 592.1 million (29.3%) lived in the Western world. The Communist world grew to 443.8 million (22%).

So Christianity is no longer a Western religion. Christianity is no longer a white man's religion. It is a world religion. During the 20th century, Christianity has become the most extensive and universal religion in history.[43]

AN EXPLOSION OF CONVERTS AND LAYMEN

Christianity has grown with increasing acceleration and rapidity in an incredible way. Dr. Kennedy had a set of statistics that he loved to quote when challenged for his optimism about the future. He called them the most encouraging statistics that he ever heard in his entire lifetime as a Christian.

> In 1900 there were 943 converts to Christ per day worldwide.
>
> That increased to 4,500 by 1950.
>
> By 1980 that grew with incredible speed to 20,000.
>
> By the end of 1994, that figure had grown to 92,000.
>
> It reached about 100,000 per day worldwide during the mid-1990s.
>
> And at last estimate, it was up to 150,000 per day by the end of this decade.

Dr. Kennedy told me he derived these statistics from the research of Dr. David Barrett, the great church statistician, who says there are 55 million new Christians per year (not counting losses through conversion to false

---

[43] David B. Barrett, *World Christian Encyclopedia: A comparative study of churches and religions in the modern world, AD 1900-2000* (New York: Oxford University Press, 1982), 3-4.

religions or through death). 55,000,000 divided by 365=150,000/per day. [44]

Dr. Ralph Winter, Chancellor of William Carey International University and past General Director for the U.S. Center for World Mission, published some amazing facts about the growth of Christianity worldwide. He states that in A.D. 100, there was one Christian for every 360 people on earth. By 1900, that number dramatically changed to 21 people for every active believer. In 2010, he lists the number as 7.3 people for every Christian believer.[45]

Thus, we see there has been the most incredible explosion of converts to Christ that the world has ever seen. Unfortunately, for us that is, most of this has taken place in other parts of the world. In Africa there were 10 million Christians in 1900; today there are roughly 400 million Christians there.[46] Similar kinds of things are happening in various places in Asia and other parts of the world.

God is at work in a tremendous way. Indeed, the Church is going forth today as an army—*"awesome as an*

---

[44] David B. Barrett and Todd M. Johnson, *World Christian Trends: Interpreting the annual Christian megacensus* (Pasadena: CA: William Carey Library, 2001).

[45] Ralph D. Winter, Phil Bogosian, Larry Boggan, Frank Markow, and Wendell Hyde, "The Amazing Countdown Facts" published by the U.S. Center for World Mission. They define a "Christian believer" as those who have been born again into a personal relationship with Jesus Christ. They list Christian believers as 800 million.

[46] David B. Barrett, *World Christian Encyclopedia: A comparative study of churches and religions in the modern world, AD 1900-2000* (New York: Oxford University Press, 1982), 4.

army with banners." That, I think, indeed, portends great things for this century.

For example, David Barrett and Todd Johnson report that 2 billion people on the planet listen to or view Christian broadcasting at least once a month. That's almost one-third the world's population. Given the present trends, Barrett and Johnson anticipate that number to climb to 2.4 billion by 2025.[47]

Barrett and Johnson also note that the percentage of Christians in the world in contrast to the world population has increased from 22.7% in 1800[48] to 33.2% in 2010. They report that 2.172 billion claim to be Christians, and they anticipate that number to rise to 2.583 billion by 2025.

They also report that the distribution of the Scriptures, in whole or in part, has exploded. In 1800, they estimate there were 500,000 Bibles being published per year. By 2010, that number had jumped to 71.4 million.[49] Indeed, the world's #1 best-seller has no true rivals.

We, in EE, have seen in the last 50 years another phenomenon. It has been the peculiar time of the layperson. An increasing tens of millions of lay people around the world have begun to share their faith in Christ. They have been equipped, trained, emboldened, and encouraged to go

---

[47] David Barrett and Todd Johnson, International Bulletin of Missionary Research, Vol. 34, No. 1.

[48] David B. Barrett and Todd M. Johnson, *World Christian Trends: Interpreting the annual Christian megacensus* (Pasadena: CA: William Carey Library, 2001), 384.

[49] David Barrett and Todd Johnson, International Bulletin of Missionary Research, Vol. 34, No. 1.

out and share the Good News with others. This is one of the reasons for the great explosion of converts around the world.

I believe that as the twenty-first century progresses, the Church is going to do things people never dreamed she would do. For one thing, we are going to continue to see the enormous growth of large churches. About 140 years ago Charles Spurgeon was considered the greatest preacher in the world. I read in the back of one of his commentaries, that that year they had received the 4,225th member into the church, making it the second largest church in Christendom. Did you grasp that? One hundred forty years ago, the second largest church in the world had 4,225 members.

Today, that would not be the second largest church in Fort Lauderdale. We have churches with tens of thousands of members here in the United States, and in some other countries they put us to shame. There is a Presbyterian church with as many as 80,000 members in Korea and another church there with 800,000 members. God is doing some incredible things.

We often hear about churches that are closing. Many of these have not been proclaiming the Gospel; they have not been winning people to Jesus Christ. So they are just withering away. But those which have been faithful to the Gospel, which have been proclaiming the Good News and training their people to do so also are going to grow. It is not going to be uncommon in the near future to see churches that have 10, 20, 50, 75 thousand members. Just a caution—church growth is not always a sign of real Christian growth, but I do believe in the growth of the true Church. Nonetheless, most of the churches that are growing so well are churches where the Gospel is being preached.

FATE OF MAINLINE CHURCHES

It is also interesting to see another change which, if things continue, will take place by the middle of the next century. The mainline churches in America will mostly have disappeared. They will be discovered to be back alleys, dead-end streets. These are those mainline denominations which have, by and large, become liberal, whose seminaries turn out ministers who do not believe the Bible —the kinds of people you have heard about in the Jesus seminar who do not believe Jesus said three-fourths of what is attributed to Him and who now reveal they do not even believe He rose from the dead.

This kind of liberal unbelief is a negative, withering, dying sort of thing. It is a plague—a blight upon the Church —and it is going to, by the grace of God, fade away.

RESURGENCE OF CHRISTIANITY

So, I believe that there will continue to be a tremendous growth in Bible-believing Christianity in this century. We saw an increase in missions in the 20th century with an increase of the number of people who have been trained and have learned to witness. I pray that soon we will see 21st century missionaries traveling all over the world, and Christians who do not witness for Christ will be the strange ducks, the rare birds. Whereas 50 years ago, when Evangelism Explosion began, it was common to find as many as 95 percent of the church members in America did not witness to anyone. By the middle of the next century, I pray that figure may be drastically altered as Christians more and more realize that it is their responsibility and their privilege to share the Gospel of Jesus Christ with others.

While we in Evangelism Explosion tend to focus on the proclamation of the Gospel (the evangelism mandate), there is a second responsibility that all of us, as Church members, are called to. We have not only been called to be light, but also salt. Light illuminates and salt preserves. Dr. Kennedy was famous for his Biblical stand for both the evangelism mandate and the cultural mandate (found in Genesis 1:28).

It's a bit alarming that many churchmen (even pastors) have no concern for the culture. There was a time when there were many advocates for the cultural mandate here in the United States (not the least of which was Dr. D. James Kennedy), but today the church seems remarkable quiet.

So, while we've seen growth in the Church worldwide, and even here in the states, there seems to be a growing disconnect with the cultural mandate.

I believe that one of strongest voices today with regard to the cultural mandate is Dr. Tony Perkins, President of the Family Research Council in Washington, D.C. Recently, while talking about the growth of the Church and our hope for the future, Tony reminded me:

> The Church has been and is growing exponentially, however, during this time of expansion the cultural and political influence of the Church has decreased almost in inverse proportion. What is missing?
>
> Perhaps the missing element is the persecution of the Church, which will prune and purify the Church making it strong and leading it to solid growth. A purified Church will be a prophetic Church, that will not just hold up the light of the Gospel but will bring the preserving power of the truth to the culture by being salt.[50]

I pray that the Church will wake up after many, many decades of lethargy and sleep. As Tony said, it might take persecution which leads to pruning and purification for that to happen. You can already feel that in the wind.

I sincerely hope that we will understand it soon and rise from that sleep to be a responsible power. Then we can reverse many of the most unfortunate and godless decisions that have been made in this country in the past few decades,

---

[50] Family Research Council is a wonderful organization located in Washington, D.C. They work diligently to preserve our Christian liberties, the family, and promote Godly government. You can find out more at: http://www.frc.org.

and America will be restored again to a Godliness which is what made us great. That is my hope and prayer.

Remember the great words attributed to Alexis de Tocqueville, but traced back to an Eisenhower speechwriter (but true, no matter who said it): "America is great because America is good. If America ever ceases to be good, America will cease to be great."

Well, we have come very close to that, but there is hope in the coming days. It isn't going to happen overnight. There are still forces of evil, godlessness, and immorality entrenched in the institutions of this nation because Christians have abdicated their responsibilities. But that, I pray, even if it requires persecution, is already beginning to change.

I'm speaking here about the United States, but I also believe and pray that same awakening will happen for the world Church.

I think that overall, the 21st century will be the most exciting time ever to be a part of the Church of Christ. It will, indeed, be fair as the moon, clear as the sun, and it will have become *"awesome as an army with banners."* And that banner over her is the love of Jesus Christ that we carry forth to a needy world. It will be a Church where members see that it is, indeed, their privilege and their holy and Godly responsibility to not merely be spectators in the pews, but to be active participants in the life of the building of the kingdom of God throughout this world. I trust that you will be a part of that glorious Church.

I hope you will think about that Heavenly Bridegroom who even now is looking for those who are truly sincere in their faith, who truly seek after holiness, who seek His face in prayer, who study His Word, and who endeavor to live for Him. To those believers, He will be unstinting and generous in His praise, and they will be those that He dearly loves. May those people be you and me.

CONCLUSION

God has great plans for His Church, and we are privileged to be a part of those plans. It is His desire that He utters those words, "Well done," to us. May God help us to live in such a way that He makes us worthy to be His Heavenly bride.

10

Watchman

(Know Your Position)

"So you, son of man: I have made you a watchman for the house of Israel; therefore you shall hear a word from My mouth and warn them for Me. When I say to the wicked, 'O wicked man, you shall surely die!' and you do not speak to warn the wicked from his way, that wicked man shall die in his iniquity; but his blood I will require at your hand."

Ezekiel 33:7-8

In 1906, the Chisso Corporation moved to Minimata, Japan—a small fishing village on Minimata Bay. In 1908, the Chisso Corporation (Chisso, in Japanese, means nitrogen) opened a large factory there and began the production of various industrial fertilizer products. In 1932, they began the production of a particular fertilizer that required the use of methyl mercury; which, after its processing, they dumped as wastewater into the bay.

This highly toxic chemical bioaccumulated in shellfish and fish in Minimata Bay and the surrounding sea. The fish were eaten by the local population, resulting in mercury poisoning. At first they noticed that small animals, like cats and dogs, began to go crazy and die unexpectedly.

On April 21, 1956, doctors examined a five-year-old girl. She had difficulty walking, difficulty speaking, and was experiencing convulsions. Two days later, her sister began exhibiting the same symptoms. Soon, eight children in that neighborhood became sick.

In general, these symptoms deteriorated and were followed by coma and death. By October 1956, 40 patients had been discovered; 14 of whom had died.

A great push came to find the cause of the illness. Soon, it became clear that the issue was mercury poisoning. Those impacted had mercury levels in their system of over 700 parts per million, indicating heavy exposure to the chemical.

By 1959, the disease and its source had been finally identified; but the company did nothing positive to change its dumping of over 6,000 tons per year of wastewater containing methyl mercury into the bay. They refused to acknowledge the danger that their actions represented to the people of Minimata and the surrounding area.

When I write that they did nothing positive, I write that because they did do something. What they did was deceive the public into thinking that they did take care of the problem. They installed a wastewater filtering plant and told the public that it removed the mercury. It did not. In a public display, the President of the Corporation drank a glass of filtered wastewater in front of the media to prove that it was safe. The stunt was an outright deception. What it did was cause the people to eat more fish, which only accelerated the contamination.

It wasn't until 1968 that the company discontinued its production and dumping of mercury into the bay. By 2001, two thousand two hundred and sixty-five victims had been officially recognized as suffering from Minimata disease (defined as a neurological syndrome cause by mercury poisoning), with over one thousand seven hundred that had died from the poisoning. Tens of thousands of people have filed lawsuits against the company, and those lawsuits and claims for compensation continue to this day.

Why do I share this awful story? Let me ask you a question. What do you think of the Chisso Corporation? If you had the opportunity to speak to one of its leaders, even its workers, what would you say?

It's not that they didn't have their reasons. The Chisso Corporation dominated this little fishing village. Taxes from this company represented over 50% of the income for the whole town. More than 25% of the town's population was employed there. Some surely felt that the ends justified the means. Do you agree? How do you feel about what they did?

I'm sure, at least to some degree, that you have a sense of righteous anger toward those that knew but said nothing (even if they had nothing to do with the process but only knew about it). They hid the truth of what was going on. And in doing so, they were wrong.

This is what we are being told by God in the passage of Scripture that we are studying. You see, if a person (a watchman) knows of a danger and does not warn the people, that watchman is guilty of the blood of those that perish.

We are told in Ezekiel 33 that God had set Ezekiel as a watchman for the house of Israel. The watchman was to stand on the tower and keep an eye on the distant horizon— watching for a cloud of dust or the glimmer of metal reflecting in the sun. If they saw a danger, they were to sound the trumpet warning the townspeople to prepare to defend themselves. If they listened to the warning, and prepared to fight, then they would be saved. If they did not listen, the fault was with them and not the watchman.

In verse 7, God shifts the focus from an external enemy to an internal issue; namely wickedness, or sin. God declares that the watchman will hear His word, and that Ezekiel must warn the people to turn from their sins.

You see that people had become convinced that their sin was not the problem. They were convinced that it was this sin of others (namely their ancestors) that was the issue. The watchman was to listen for God's word, then tell the people that God said they were wicked and that they would surely die.

Ezekiel must have been really taken back by God's words. I mean think about it: God was basically telling him that he could (that one possibility was that he might) fail at the task God had given him. God warned in verse 8, *"When I say to the wicked, 'O wicked man, you shall surely die!' and you do not speak to warn the wicked from his way, that wicked man shall die in his iniquity; but his blood I will require at your hand."* Wow. If he simply heard this first part, he would surely have been filled with absolute dread.

But God continues with a promise—a comfort of grand dimension. In verse 9 God said, *"Nevertheless if you warn the wicked to turn from his way, he does not turn from his way, he shall die in his iniquity; but you have delivered your soul."* Bottom-line, "Ezekiel, you can do the job. It's possible for you. And it's not up to you what they decide. Just do your job, and I'll handle the rest." That's what God said.

Ezekiel had a duty. That duty was specific. God established punishment and rewards depending on what Ezekiel did. Ezekiel had to be open to receive the message and be willing to speak. Silence, in this case, was not golden.

There are several things we can learn from this message.

First, the job description for a watchmen is specific and set by God Himself.

Second, it is God's message; it's not up to the watchman to decide what to proclaim.

Third, the results are up to God; the watchman cannot make people believe and act.

Fourth, it is possible for the watchman to either do, or not do, the job. But the bottom line is, it is the watchman that is in jeopardy. The watchman is the one at risk.

This is basically the same warning that Mordecai gave to Esther when he said (and I'm paraphrasing here), *"Don't get it into your head that God will not save His people. But if you remain silent at this time, you and your family will be destroyed. And how do you know that you were not born for such a time as this?"* (Esther 4:13)

It's a powerful story. God speaks. The people need to be warned or their blood is on the hands of the watchman, and God established the watchman to do the warning.

Now here's the kicker: God has made each and every one of us who bear the name of Christ a watchman.

For the Christian, for the one who trusts in Jesus Christ alone for eternal life, his or her purpose is not elective. Our purpose in life is set by Christ Himself. He told us in Mark 16:15, *"Go into all the world and preach the gospel to every creature."* In Acts 1:8, Jesus said, *"...you shall be witnesses to Me in Jerusalem, and in all Judea and Samaria, and to the end of the earth."*

The apostle Paul tells us in 2 Corinthians 5:17-20,

Therefore, if anyone is in Christ, he is a new creation; old things have passed away; behold, all things have become new. 18 Now all things are of God, who has reconciled us to Himself through Jesus Christ, and has given us the ministry of reconciliation, 19 that is, that God was in Christ reconciling the world to Himself, not imputing their trespasses to them, and has committed to us the word of reconciliation. Now then, we are ambassadors for Christ, as though God were pleading through us: we implore you on Christ's behalf, be reconciled to God."

You see, God tells us that we (all of us who are saved) are ambassadors, as if He were pleading through us, "Be reconciled to Christ."

There is no more important work that we can do. I must say, that as President of Evangelism Explosion, I am sometimes a bit discouraged over how few Christians witness. Dr. Kennedy stated, in the book *Evangelism Explosion*, that 95% of Christians never lead anyone to Christ.[51] Why?

Before I answer that question, I think its important to clarify what I mean by the word "witness". Recently, a study by the Barna Group stated that 65% of evangelical Christians witnessed last year.[52] It seems rather unlikely

---

[51] D. James Kennedy, *Evangelism Explosion*, page 4.

[52] Taken from the Barna Group website in an article titled, "Survey Shows How Christians Share Their Faith", dated January 31, 2005.

that 65% could witness but not lead anyone (or very few) to the Lord, doesn't it? The reason for this dilemma is how one defines this word "witness".

C.S. Lewis, in his book *Mere Christianity*, starts out by talking about the definition of the word "Christian". He makes the case that over time people have changed the word "Christian" because they do not like its meaning.[53] This is what we are doing with the word "witness", or "evangelism". When Barna's survey talks about 65% of evangelical Christians witnessing, their definition is nothing more than bringing up some Christian ideal or brief testimony into the conversation. In fact, they clearly state that most younger Christians will not engage in any conversation regarding moral values. When we use the word witness in this book, we are referring to the actual sharing of the Gospel with people who have not yet heard. This, of course, deals with grace, the condition of man in sin, the nature of God towards sin, the work of Jesus in redemption, and the necessity of trust in that saving work of Christ. So then, why is it that so few Christians are willing to share this important truth with their friends, relatives, work associates, and neighbors?

In truth, I think that there are a lot of reasons. I'll just name a few.

One is that we get involved in all kinds of seemingly good things that keep us all too busy. Jim Collins wrote a

---

[53] C.S. Lewis, *Mere Christianity* (New York, NY: HarperSanFrancisco, 1980).

widely used book in the business world called *Good to Great*. He opens the popular book with this statement, "Good is the enemy of great."[54] So many times we get involved in all kinds of good things; and yet, they are not the great thing that we could be doing in seeing men and women come to call Jesus Lord and Savior. Christ said, *"If you love Me, keep My commandments."* (John 14:15). His last command should be out first concern.

Another reason is, and this may sound harsh, sometimes we don't care. I was in the Middle East recently and I commented to an elder, "Why don't Christians witness to Arab Muslims? Don't they care that they will spend eternity in Hell?" The elder responded, "Well, brother, between you and me, that's probably the best place for them." Now that may be more boldly said than we would be comfortable with, but isn't it at least a little bit true about how we feel about some people?

A third reason, and the last that I'll mention, is sin in our lives. It is hard for us to go tell others what they should believe when we see the sins we commit. The great Charles Spurgeon added another thought to this. He said that sin will result in no fruit, which will frustrate our efforts and squelch our desire to witness. He said, "If I, as God's minister, have no conversions, I dare not attribute the fact to divine sovereignty. It may be so, but I am always afraid to make divine sovereignty that scapegoat for my iniquities.

---

[54] Jim Collins, *Good to Great* (New York, NY: HarperCollins, 2001) 1.

I rather think that if God withholds the blessing, there is a cause; and may not the cause be in myself, that I do not live as near to God as I should, or am indulging in something His holy eyes cannot look upon? I speak to you who are church members, if in your personal Bible study, your witnessing, or if in any other work you are doing, you do not win souls to God, cry unto Him, 'Search me, O God, and know my heart; try me, and know my thoughts; and see if there be any wicked way in me; and lead me in the way everlasting.' Sin blocks up the channel of mercy."[55]

The shame is that we live on a planet with slightly more than 2 billion,[56] living in over 6,800 people groups, who have never been warned by anyone.[57] They live in a culture, or a people group, that has no one who has ever heard the name of Jesus. And unless something changes, they will never have the opportunity to hear.

But the good news is that things are changing. Do you realize how simple it would be to reach the world for Jesus Christ if every one of the professing Christians became part of the army and started witnessing to their friends, relatives, work associates, and neighbors? There is something like one billion evangelical Christians on this earth. Now, if one billion people all shared the gospel and

---

[55] Charles Spurgeon, "Joshua's Vision" preached February 16, 1868.

[56] David Barrett and Todd Johnson, International Bulletin of Missionary Research, Vol. 34, No. 1.

[57] "Joshua Project." August 13, 2010. http://joshuaproject.net.

led only one person to the Lord in an entire year, the next year there would be two billion Christians. And what if we did it the second year? There would be four billion Christians. And what if we did it the third year? There would be...well...we don't have that many people on earth —we'd have to get busy making more people so we could get to the eight billion. In three years time, we could reach the world for Christ if we could just engage every layperson. Laypeople can do amazing things.

I know one layperson who liked to go to prisons. He would go to this one particular prison and lead Bible studies for the thirty Christians out of a thousand inmates in that prison. He was diligent and kept going every week to share with those thirty. Well one day, he decided to train those thirty Christians to witness for Jesus Christ. You know how many Christians there are today in that prison? The day that I was there, there were over four hundred of the thousand that were Bible-believing Christians. The guards were hugging me and saying, "What a wonderful change has happened in this prison." All because a layperson committed to doing what the Bible said and applied it in his life.

Here is another example. Not to long ago, I was in northern Vietnam, near the border of China. I met a layperson who had a passion for one of the least reached people groups on earth—the Yau people group. He gathered up a few Christians and taught them to share their faith through EE. The Sunday morning I was there I spoke to over 400 Christians that had been led to the Lord by the faithful few who were trained in EE. You could not fit any more people into the large hut where they were meeting. Even though they are extremely poor people, they took up a collection to buy 80 sets of EE training materials to train all the leaders in the church to witness for Christ. They told me, "We tried to witness before but never could. Now we lead people to Christ everyday!" They introduced me to two men from another tribe who had just come to Christ through EE. They were the first two Christians of another "unreached" people group. All of this started with a few laypeople who had a vision for change.

But it is not just the people in prison or in distant, remote locations like Vietnam who need to hear the gospel. The shame is that some who have never really heard are right here within our families, workplaces, friendships, and neighborhoods.

As we recorded video for our new XEE product, we interviewed a young man who is the lead singer for a Christian group named Revive. They recently opened up for Third Day all across America. Dave, this lead singer, said to me, "Imagine one of your good friends saying to you, 'Hold on a moment. Why didn't you ever tell me about this? I thought you cared for me!'"

Well, I don't have to imagine it. One day, Ann and I were walking around the block with our children. One of

Josh's friends, named Cody, came with us. As we were walking, Cody said, "My mom doesn't live here anymore." Talk about a gut punch...

That night, I saw his dad, Bill, sitting on his front porch. I went over to talk to him. I said, "Bill, Jesus can fix this. He is the most important person in my life. Jesus has made me new." Bill looked me straight in the eye and said, "John, you are a liar."

After I picked myself up off the ground, he continued. "When you got a new car, you took me for a ride the same day. When anything exciting happened in your life, you told me right away. Now you're telling me that Jesus is the most important person in your life and you are just now telling me? That can't be right."

I agreed. It wasn't right. I apologized and asked Bill to forgive me. We then spent the next eight weeks going through a Bible study and then the Gospel. Bill gave his heart to Christ and became a new man. God has saved his family, restored his marriage, and given him new hope.

This passage in Ezekiel tells us that we can do it. We can become the watchman we were meant to be. We can hear the Word of the Lord and become not merely hearers of the Word, but doers of the Word as well. You can share Christ with your friends, relatives, work associates, and neighbors. You can be all that God has called you to be. I believe it, and God believes it—it is why He gave you the position in the first place.

What is your mission? What is your purpose? Have you heard the call of God upon your life to become the witness He has called you to be? Let me assure you that there is no greater joy than that of seeing people come into a right relationship with God through the wonderful work of Jesus Christ on the cross. And there has never been a more important time for you to be involved. God is doing some amazing things...

We recently conducted a weeklong EE Leadership Training Clinic in Northern Iraq. Pastors there had been requesting for over two years that we come and equip them in EE. In one week, we trained seventy-five people from ten churches all over Iraq. We witnessed to over two hundred fifty people and had one hundred fifty-seven pray to receive Christ and agree to be publicly baptized.

Two days later a mob of Muslims stormed into the pastor's home and beat his father to death right in front of his family. Then they said, "If you keep this up, we'll kill your children next." The pastor wrote me a few weeks later and said, "Don't think this was a mistake. We've already begun EE. We'll train everyone. If they want to stop us, they'll have to kill us all." Some might say that the death of the pastor's father was a tragedy. But Dr. Kennedy would not have agreed. He would have said, "No. A tragedy is when someone lives a full life and never does anything for Jesus."

In 1985, Dr. Kennedy delivered a message from the pulpit. He encouraged all in attendance by saying,

> God has called us to be co-laborers with Himself, the living Triune God, in the emancipation of the souls of men in bringing them the gift of everlasting life. He made us, and He bought us with a great price. We were redeemed, not with silver and gold, but with the precious blood of Jesus Christ. At infinite cost, upon the cross, Christ paid for our sins and purchased our redemption and offers now eternal life to those that will trust in Him.
>
> To all of us who have placed our trust in Him, we are twice His, made and redeemed for a glorious purpose. It is a purpose that will cause your pulse to quicken and your blood to race through your veins, to think that you can have a part with the Eternal God in the redemption of the world.
>
> What could be a more glorious purpose and meaning for life than that? Dear friend, what is the purpose of your life?"

Do you remember how you felt about the Chisso Corporation for their keeping news to themselves? News that for the lack of hearing caused great harm to many people? Let us not allow such things to be said about us. It would be far better to not appoint a watchman than to appoint one that is unfaithful to his or her task.

CONCLUSION

The need is urgent. The time is pressing. The duty is clear. My dear friend, you matter in this great work. You can do it. You can be the witness that Jesus Christ has called you to be.

11

Brave Heart

(Know Your Power)

"Therefore, since we have this ministry, as we have received mercy, we do not lose heart."

2 Corinthians 4:1

About nine years ago, I was playing a computer game with my kids called "Galactic Battlegrounds" based on the Star Wars model. We like it because it is a game of good versus evil (we, of course, were on the good side), and four of us can play at the same time. You can interact with one another while fighting off the bad guys.

At one point I noticed our son Joshua, who was ten years old at the time, had become very quiet. When I looked at his section of the screen, I noticed the enemy was annihilating him. My then nine-year-old daughter Hannah must have noticed it at the same time. She cried out, "Josh, do you want us to come help?" But Josh discouragingly replied, "No, don't bother. They've already destroyed everything that's worth saving. It's over." You could hear it in his voice. You could recognize it in his words. You could see it in his countenance when he trudged out of his room. He had given up. He had lost hope. He had lost heart.

That was just a game, but you know it happens in real life. There was a man named Jerry. He had been diagnosed with Multiple Myeloma—bone cancer. He had been given two to six months to live. Then the Red Cross told him that they were working on an experimental cure for the disease. If he could only hold on, the cure would come. And hold on he did. When six months came around, he was doing very well. After a year, he looked good. Two years later, he was still hanging on.

But then the first day of December the Red Cross called again and said that the cure was not ready. He would not make it. Crushed, Jerry died seventeen days later. He had lost hope. He had lost heart.

It seems that hope is such a vital thing. How do we get it? How do we keep it in such troubled times when we are tested and tried? How is it that we maintain hope to keep doing the work God has called us to do?

Many of us have been through difficult times, and we need encouragement. There is certainly enough trouble and disappointment in life to get us down, and we need to be constantly reminded of God's love for us and His promises to us.

As I thought through and prayed through this problem of losing heart or losing hope in troubled times, God showed me a beautiful passage of Scripture about how you and I can have hope—how we can have brave hearts.

The Apostle Paul wrote to the Christians at Corinth all about how God has shown His mercy to us, given us His message, and that whatever problems we may have are but momentary and fleeting. In this chapter, we will consider three marvelous truths from 2 Corinthians 4, truths that instill hope for those who are committed to Jesus Christ and the spread of His Gospel.

When we get beat up by the circumstances of life, it seems natural to withdraw for healing or to hide and get away. But 2 Corinthians 4 tells us that this thinking, although it feels right, is actually backwards if we want to keep hope and keep heart. It says in verse 1, "Because, since we have this ministry, we do not lose heart." The reason we do not lose heart is that we have been given a ministry. What ministry? Well, hopefully you know what ministry we have because we studied it in the previous chapter of this book. It is this idea that we have been made ambassadors for Christ, that we are reconciling the world to God through Christ Jesus, and that we are going and pleading with people, "Be reconciled with God." Paul tells us exactly this in the next chapter of Scripture, 2 Corinthians 5:

> *Now all things are of God, who has reconciled us to Himself through Jesus Christ, and has given us the ministry of reconciliation, that is, that God was in Christ*

reconciling the world to Himself, not imputing their trespasses to them, and has committed to us the word of reconciliation. Now then, we are ambassadors for Christ, as though God were pleading through us: we implore you on Christ's behalf, be reconciled to God (2 Corinthians 5:18-20).

Because we have this ministry, we do not lose hope. Our hope has nothing to do with our circumstances, nothing to do with how we feel, and nothing to do with what people think about us or say about us. Our hope comes from the fact that God has given us this ministry.

Let us examine 2 Corinthians 4 to understand how God gives us this hope.

MERCY

We have this ministry by God's mercy. In 4:1, Paul declares: *"Therefore, since we have this ministry, as we have received mercy, we do not lose heart."*

Everyone who has received God's mercy has this ministry. You cannot have one without the other. The two go together, hand in hand. Do you recall when it was that you first experienced God's mercy?

I do. You have already heard my story that started in the fall of 1989. You heard how God led me into the office of Dr. Tom Stebbins who asked me if I knew for sure I was going to Heaven. I said, "No. Can a person know that?"

He asked me, "If you die tonight and stand before God and He asks you, "Why should I let you into my Heaven?" what would you say?" It was there in his office on that Monday that I heard the Gospel of Jesus Christ, and I understood what it was to trust in Jesus. That very day my life was changed, and I have never been the same. Not long after that day I got trained in Evangelism Explosion (EE)— again, a church visitation ministry founded by Dr. Kennedy and used worldwide, whereby lay people are trained and then train others in how to share their faith in Christ. So not long after my conversion, through EE, I began to share my faith.

What an adventure! Now I get to be part of the greatest GO-mission on earth, the ministry of reconciling lost people to Christ. There is nothing more thrilling. "Rescue the perishing. Duty demands it." When you understand what Paul is telling us here, this hymn by Fannie Crosby will stir you up.[58]

You see how the two are tied together? You cannot have hope without God's mercy. With God's mercy comes God's ministry.

But it is more than that. God has not only given us a ministry to do because He is given us the mercy of salvation, but also He has given us a ministry to do because He is merciful to us.

---

[58] Rescue the Perishing was written by Fannie Crosby in 1869 and appeared in *Songs of Devotion* (New York: Biglow & Main) in 1870.

As we minister, we are strengthened. We are made whole. How many times have I been tired and weary coming to EE, physically beat down? Yet, after actually going out and experiencing divinely appointed encounters helping lead people to faith in Jesus Christ, I became revitalized. I felt great afterwards and was so glad I went, even though before going, I was tempted to not go that night. I am so glad I ignored that voice that said, "It doesn't matter if you miss just this one night. Besides, you're so tired, and you normally work so hard for the Lord, yada, yada, yada." But I obeyed and; after obeying, I felt renewed.

How often have we seen people retire; and soon after, they die? We were born to have purpose and meaning in our lives. God has given us this meaning through His infinite mercy.

Mercy. We receive it first through salvation and then through accepting and doing His ministry of reconciliation.

MESSAGE

We accomplish this ministry by proclaiming God's message:

> *For we do not preach ourselves, but Christ Jesus the Lord, and ourselves your bondservants for Jesus' sake. For it is God who commanded light to shine out of darkness, who has shone in our hearts to give the light of*

the knowledge of the glory of God in the face of Jesus Christ (2 Corinthians 4:5-6).

Now, there are a few things that we need to see about this message.

The first thing to note is that it is not our message. It is God's. It is not about us, it is about Jesus.

There is a story about a man who became very good at making things out of dirt. In fact, he got so good at making things out of dirt that he got to the place where he could make pure energy out of dirt. With pure energy he could make virtually anything else. One day, after he had become very full of himself, he went to God and challenged Him saying, "Let's have a contest and see who can make the best thing out of dirt."

God said, "Okay." So the man reached down to get a handful of dirt, but God quickly stopped him saying, "Hey, get your own dirt."

Sometimes we begin to imagine that it is our own message. We begin to tinker with it and say, "Well, the world needs this, or they need to hear that, or surely we can't say that to people!" But it is not our message: it is God's message. And what a wonderful thing that is. If I had to go out and proclaim me to the world, there would be many times that I would be too embarrassed to do that. I have no message of my own.

Before I was saved, I was a disc jockey at a rock-and-roll radio station. The station was irreverent and rebellious.

Not much of an example for the kids of the community. Right after I became a Christian, I got trained in Evangelism Explosion. Sometimes we would go up to a door; and the people would say, "Hey, aren't you that guy on the radio? I came to one of your beer parties." Had we been there to tell them about me, we would have been done. Game over. Pack up and go home. But, praise God, we were not there to tell them about me. We were there to tell them about Jesus. And Jesus saves even guys like me. That is the miracle!

I once had a chance to take a group of people to India on a short-term mission trip. We were teaching an Evangelism Explosion clinic there in the town of New Delhi. One day I noticed a plaque in the corner of the entryway. On it was 2 Corinthians 4:6: *"For it is God who commanded light to shine out of darkness, who has shone in our hearts to give the light of the knowledge of the glory of God in the face of Jesus Christ."* Looking past the plaque and out the window, there was a building dedicated to oppressing the message of Christianity and keeping the Hindu religion the official religion of India. It bothered me every day, because we would go out to share the gospel; and we would run into so many people who had never even heard of Jesus before. One day, I was praying to God as I memorized this verse, "God, you commanded light to shine into darkness, but look! It hasn't made it here yet."

And then it felt like God hit me with a baseball bat. Bam! "It was you I commanded, not the light. I commanded you to go take the light into the darkness."

There is great darkness there. So many of the people that we shared with had never even heard of Jesus in their life, yet God has commanded His light to shine. Many men and women are going and sharing the gospel of Jesus Christ, and it is making a difference in India. People are coming to Christ all through that nation. Isn't it wonderful that we have a message that God has given us that is not our message but is His message, and it makes a difference across cultures and generations? It changes lives. His message is going forth.

Not only is it God's message, but it is God's power as well. In 2 Corinthians 4:7, it says, *"But we have this treasure in earthen vessels, that the excellence of the power may be of God and not of us."*

When we start talking about going out and telling people about Jesus, someone always says, "I can't do it." I always say, "You're right, and praise God you know that. But God can and will do it through you." The whole point is that sharing the Gospel will be done by people who cannot do it so that everyone will see that God did it.

Sometimes we as Christians forget the power that is at work in us, through God the Spirit. Chuck Swindoll, in his book *Flying Close to the Flame*, gave us a list of the differences that God's power makes in our lives. It is shocking to hear how much power we have to live differently than the world. These things are true of you if you are a Christian:

I am in Christ.
I live with Him and He lives with me.
I know the relief of bring cleansed from personal sin.
I am able to live without sin's dominating control.
I have immediate access to the Father through prayer.
I can understand the Scriptures.
I am able to forgive—and should forgive—whoever wrongs me.
I have the capacity to bear fruit, daily, continually, routinely.
I possess at least one (sometimes more than one) spiritual gift.
I worship with joy and with purpose.
I find the church vital, not routine or boring.
I have a faith to share with others.
I love and need other people.
I look forward to having close fellowship with fellow Christians.
I am able to obey the teaching of the Word of God.
I continue to learn and grow toward maturity.
I can endure suffering and hardship without losing heart.
I depend and trust in my Lord for daily strength and provisions.
I can know God's will.
I live in anticipation of Christ's return.

I have the assurance of Heaven after I die.[59]

What power we possess in Christ. We have God's power to do God's ministry.

However, we need to understand that God's message always brings about conflict; because God's message is, in and of itself, confrontational. It will be a struggle for us to proclaim it.

You hear people all the time talking about "non-confrontational evangelism." What they really mean is non-evangelism. The Gospel itself is confrontational. Now in EE, we do our best to not add confrontation to the message by our actions and words, as some do. But still, there is no way around it—the Gospel is a confrontational message. The Gospel says, "You are a sinner. You have broken God's commands, and God is not OK with that." However, the Good News is that Jesus gave His life, so we can be whole.

The proclamation of the Good News in Scripture is not presented as a cakewalk:

We are hard-pressed on every side, yet not crushed; we are perplexed, but not in despair; persecuted, but not forsaken; struck down, but not destroyed (2 Corinthians 4:8-9).

---

[59] Charles R. Swindoll, *Flying Close to the Flame* (Dallas et al: Word Publishing, 1993), 243.

Why should this surprise us? Jesus said, *"In the world you will have tribulation; but be of good cheer, I have overcome the world"* (John 16:33). We cannot avoid troubles. God allows trials to come. But they always bring about our growth. James says that, *"...the testing of your faith produces patience (or endurance)"* (1:3).

Listen to what Peter said in 1 Peter 4:19: *"Therefore let those who suffer according to the will of God commit their souls to Him in doing good, as to a faithful Creator."*

Even though in 2 Corinthians God tells us we will be hard pressed on every side, He follows with, *"All this is for your benefit, so that the grace that is reaching more and more people may cause thanksgiving to overflow to the glory of God. Therefore we do not lose heart"* (2 Corinthians 4:15-16).

We can take comfort in the fact that it is God's message (not our own), delivered in His power; and even the struggle to deliver it is His struggle.

MOMENT

Finally, we see that we have this ministry for but a moment:

> *For our light affliction, which is but for a moment, is working for us a far more exceeding and eternal weight of glory, while we do not look at the things which are seen, but at the things which are not seen. For the things*

*which are seen are temporary, but the things which are
not seen are eternal* (2 Corinthians 4:17-18).

Remember that our affliction comes as we do God's
ministry. However, our affliction, and therefore our
ministry, is but for a moment.

The truth is that we think we have all the time in the
world, but we do not. We could fill the rest of the day with
stories of people who thought they had all kinds of time,
but they did not. We need only to remember 9-11 to know
it is true.[60] Do you have loved ones that need to hear about
Jesus? Friends that need to know of Christ? Work
associates or neighbors that need to hear? Do not put it off.
We have this ministry right now. Today is the day of
salvation.[61]

Have you ever thought about what you will be doing in
Heaven? I am sure there are lots of things you would like to
do. My wife wants to be God's gardener. I think she would
be very good at that. But I can tell you one thing that you
will not be able to do. That is, you will never be able to
witness to someone and have them accept Jesus Christ as
their Savior and Lord. This is the day God has given us for
that. This is the day of salvation! We must gain an eternal

---

[60] Referring to the attacks against the United States by terrorists on September 11, 2001. More
information at: http://en.wikipedia.org/wiki/September_11_attacks.

[61] 2 Corinthians 6:2.

perspective. We must, as Paul tells us, focus on the things not seen.

The writer to the Hebrews tells us that faith is the evidence of things not seen.[62] Because of God's Word, we can believe things that make no sense to our eyes. Through God's Word, we can gain a proper eternal perspective on money (treasures in Heaven), time (only what is done for Christ will last), energy (we do not labor in vain), and talent (our best is for the Lord's glory).

But we are told that there is a timeframe in which this must be done—today.

God's mercy, message, and moment ultimately lead us to, and flow from, God's ministry. And when we have God's ministry we have a life of purpose and hope. And we will have brave hearts.

Earlier, I told you a story about a man named Jerry who had Multiple Myeloma. I wish that I could tell you that that was a story that I had heard. It was not. Jerry was my dad. I was there that day when I saw hope leave. It was really one of the saddest days of my life.

Hope is so critical. With hope, we can act bravely, against all odds. Though we are broken to pieces with miseries and calamities, we will not yield. Isaiah 40:31 says this (paraphrase), *"They that hope in the Lord will renew their strength, and they will soar on wings like eagles."* Now it probably uses "wait" in your Bible; but it is the

---

[62] Hebrews 11:1.

same Hebrew word that is used for hope. How do you feel today? Do you have a brave heart? Are you filled with hope?

There was a movie called *Brave Heart* directed by and starring Mel Gibson. He played a poor Scotsman whose wife had been killed by the nobles in league with the British Crown. In this movie he rallied all of Scotland to stand up against what seemed an overwhelming foe to fight for freedom. Throughout the fight, and even to his last breath, he held on to the hope of freedom. Hope made him brave. Hope gave him heart.

Heart. An all-consuming passion. The end-all, be-all of our lives.

Consider more of what God has to say:

"I shall see [Him] for myself, and my eyes shall behold, and not another. How my heart yearns within me!" (Job 19:27).

"My soul faints for Your salvation, but I hope in Your word" (Psalm 119:81).

"My flesh and my heart may fail; but God is the strength of my heart and my portion forever" (Psalm 73:26).

CONCLUSION

Do you want a brave heart today? If you have received His mercy, have you accepted your responsibility within His ministry to bring the lost to Christ? As you minister, you will have hope. As you minister, you will have a brave heart. May it ever be said of us that we were men and women of great hope, men and women with brave hearts.

12

A New Heaven and
A New Earth

(Know Your Promises)

"Now I saw a new heaven and a new earth, for the first heaven and the first earth had passed away. Also there was no more sea."

Revelation 21:1

Hope—the vital ingredient for a successful life. "Without hope," said William Carey, the founder of the modern missionary movement as he went to India, "it is impossible to carry on indefinitely any great enterprise."[63]

Thomas Carlyle tells us that they asked of John Knox, the great reformer and transformer of Scotland, as he lay dying on his bed: "Hast thou hope?" He spoke not a word, but lifted his finger to Heaven, and so he died.[64]

---

[63] William Carey actively served in India for forty-one years until his death at the age of seventy-three in 1834. The way was hard, but he persevered and paved the way for missionarys to come. In his words, "Expect great things from God. Attempt great things for God."

[64] Rev. Elon Foster, D.D., *New Cyclopaedia of Prose Illustrations* (New York, NY: Funk & Wagnalls Company, 1872) Volumer 1, 357. Entry 3051 by Thomas Carlyle.

Hope—that essential element for continued effort toward any great goal. *"My flesh,"* said David, *"...will rest in hope"* (Psalm 16:9). Can you say that? It depends upon your faith, because faith looks back and anchors itself to the Cross and gives life to a hope, which looks forward to a crown.

"Hope is never ill when faith is well," said the extraordinary John Bunyan.[65]

Even William Shakespeare, the bard from Stratford on Avon, said, "My hopes in Heaven dwell."[66]

Yet, sad to say, most people in this world live and die without hope. Hundreds of millions of Hindus, not to mention hundreds of millions of Buddhists, have no real or substantial hope at all. For them, their lives are caught and chained to the circling wheel of reincarnation. Over and over again they are dipped back into the misery and woe of this life, only at length, thousands of lives later, to finally reach the blessed goal...of what? Of extinction of all personal consciousness, when, like a drop of rain, they fall back into the great ocean and consciousness is no more.

And so, such hopeless lives are also lived in the West by millions of Humanists and Atheists and Secularists and even millions of students in our schools who have been

---

[65] John Bunyan, *The Whole Works of John Bunyan* (London: W.G. Blackie and Co., Printers, 1862) Volume 1, 583.

[66] William Shakespeare, *The Works of William Shakespeare* (Boston: Munroe & Francis, 1811) Volume 6, 66.

robbed and rifled of all hope by such unbelievers. And so, suicide is a leading cause of death among college-aged students today because their lives have no hope.

But, marvelous to tell, Jesus Christ has given to us the only real and substantial hope that the world knows. He has given to us this great hope when He spoke those wondrous words which have sung their way into myriads of bereft hearts down through the centuries: *"In my Father's house are many mansions; if it were not so, I would have told you. I go to prepare a place for you"* (John 14:2). What a marvelous hope was thus unfolded.

The Apostle John, the closest to the bosom of Christ, in the last two chapters of his great Revelation, pulls the curtains aside for a few moments to reveal for us at least some glimpse of that glory which is to come. *"Now I saw a new heaven and a new earth, for the first heaven and the first earth had passed away...Then I, John, saw the holy city, New Jerusalem, coming down out of heaven from God, prepared as a bride adorned for her husband"* (Revelation 21:1-2).

What a glorious hope that is. Are these marvelous pictures which he paints, having dipped his hand into all of the colors of the earthly beauty and Heavenly light, to be taken literally, or are they merely symbols? For he has taken the most magnificent and matchless beauties known to man and has used them to paint the picture of the Holy City, New Jerusalem. If this is not the reality, but merely a pale picture of some greater reality, then it is beyond the ability of human tongue and speech to declare.

How glorious must that new Heaven and new earth be. Imagine yourself on a transparent crystalline morning, where the sunlight beams brightly and everything seems to be more alive, when there is a slight chill and yet a warmth from the sun. How could anyone improve on such a beautiful day in this life? And yet, it shall be as nothing, for *"Eye has not seen, nor ear heard, nor have entered into the heart of man the things which God has prepared for those who love Him"* (1 Corinthians 2:9).

How wonderful He is to create a new Heaven and a new earth—the final abode of the redeemed—a whole new creation made for His beloved. What a threshold our Husband, our Bridegroom, will carry us over in that glorious day into the city of our God—that city which all of the Old Testament saints looked for and sought and died without seeing; that city that Abraham sought for; that city that had foundations covered with precious jewels; that city not made with human hands, but a city whose builder and maker is God Himself.

We have seen some of the wonders of human architecture and building. But what must that city whose Maker and Builder is Almighty God be like? First we are told that in that matchless city not merely the streets, but the buildings, the towers, and the spires are made of pure gold, clear as glass—transparent gold. What magnificence is thereby portrayed for us in such a city as this.

THE GLORY OF GOD

The very first thing we are told about it is that it will have the glory of God, and its light will be like a transparent jasper stone. Now today the average jasper is opaque. But the ancient stone, about which the apostle speaks, was one that was clear as crystal, either blue or green, depending on the locale from which it was taken. So shall be the glory of God that overshines this city made of transparent gold.

What a marvelous place it must be—a city whose foundations and walls are made of precious stones in which there are many things that we have never seen or dreamt of, and yet many things we know quite well will not be found there at all.

There will be no sun and no moon, for the glory and brightness of God Almighty and the Lamb shall be the light of it.

There will be no need for artificial lighting, for there will be no night there.

How will you sleep? You will not sleep at all. But you object that we grow weary at times and need to rest. Yes, but that is here in the city of man, but in the city of God, you will never grow weary.

Your energy will never flag; your enthusiasm will never dampen; you will never need rest in that time. You will be filled with a boundless energy beyond anything ever that you have known, in a perfect body that knows no limitations. You shall dwell forever with Him.

There will be no temple or church in that city, for the Lamb and the Lord God Almighty are the temple thereof. You come to church because you cannot see the face of God. There you shall see the very face of the Almighty, and live—forever.

There will be no need of mediation in that day, for then you may talk with the Living Christ or the Father Himself.

There will be no more death nor sorrow nor sadness nor pain. For many, I am sure, to be delivered forever from all pain would be Heaven itself. There are many who hardly ever know a day when they are not in acute pain. What leaping and running for joy will happen in that day when some of you now, who can hardly take a step without your knees or hips or back or neck or head aching, will be able to run and leap as you have never run and leaped before.

There will be no more sea. There is another place, and it is a sea, but not the kind of sea that you would want to sail upon; for it is a sea of fire.

But, I think that here, as almost everywhere, John is being symbolic again. The "sea" in his circumstances, and to the ancients, was not a place of amusement and joy as it is to us today, but, rather, it was a place of mystery and a place of death. Ships never sailed beyond the sight of land. There was no compass; there was no chart; the shallows were not marked; there were no buoys or life stations; and few would risk their lives upon the sea.

For John, the sea was a means of separation. He had been banished to the island of Patmos. From there he looked across the angry waves of that sea to where all of his friends and children in the Lord dwelt. Oh, that the sea might be removed and he might join again those whom he had loved and lost. Separation is one of the greatest pains of this world. Well, there will be no more separation in that day, for there will be no more sea.

There is a marvelous and wonderful directory—The Lamb's Book of Life—that you may use in that city of God. In it are inscribed the names of those who have trusted in Christ, the Lamb of God that takes away the sin of the world.

Do you know for sure that your name is written there? If you do not, then I would urge you, even now, to make sure. You know not what a day may bring forth. This could be your last day upon this earth, the last opportunity that you will have, the last person whose voice urges you to come to Him whose arms are widespread inviting you. *"Come to me...and I will give you rest."* (Matthesw 11:28). Rest and joy.

And that joy will be but a foretaste of the joy that will be yours forever. For He will not wipe our tears away with His own hands merely to let them break forth afresh again. It will be the end of grieving, and causes of tears and sadness and sorrow shall be removed, and there shall be no more sorrow, nor pain, nor suffering, nor separation, nor death. It will be not only the end of grief, but it will also be the beginning of joy; not only the ending of the lamentation, but also the beginning of a song of victory.

CONCLUSION

How glorious that will be when in the place of the dimness of tears, there is seen a sparkle of joy and you will stand like a conqueror—one who has overcome the world, the flesh, and the devil by the grace of God and by the blood of the Lamb. You will stand plumed with a crest of triumph, full in the undimmed glory of Immanuel's smile. You will sing a new song forever and sway with gladness ever fresh, amidst fountains that dance like diamonds, and rivers and streams that go laughingly on for eternity. You will lift up your voices and together you will shout.

You will look not upon the Victim's bloody cross, but upon the Victor's blazing crown. There will rise from every throat the shout of "Hallelujah!" and "Hosannah!" to Him that sits upon the throne. Thus, in everlasting joy, you will live forever with your Lord. *"I the LORD have spoken it."* (Ezekiel 24:14). It is certain and sure and is written with figures of light. Death will be no more and we will live with Him forever and ever.

Soli Deo Gloria!

FINISH

Part III

13

Finishing Strong

(Show Who You Really Are)

"...let us run with endurance the race that is set before us, looking unto Jesus, the author and finisher of our faith..."

Hebrews 12:1-2

He was old and feeble when I first saw him coming up the aisle. Laboring on his cane, he slowly but surely made his way up to talk to me. I had just finished speaking at a convention where I had encouraged everyone to get involved in witnessing. As I watched him make his way I thought to myself, "Why is this man coming to talk to me?"

When he got to the front, Robert put his finger up into my face, and he exclaimed, "Young man, I've tried witnessing for Jesus Christ my entire life, and I've never led anyone to Jesus. And now you tell me that if I get involved in this 'EE thing' that I could to lead someone to Christ before I die!" Well, as I said, Robert looked pretty feeble. But I replied, "Yes! I believe that if you get involved, you will lead someone to Jesus before you die.

But you know what? It's not my job to do that. It's your pastor's job to do train you. You need to go home and ask your pastor on Sunday to equip you to witness for Jesus Christ."

My phone was ringing when I walked in the door on Monday morning. I picked it up, and it was Robert Strickler from Freehold, New Jersey. And he said, "You know what my pastor said? He said, 'No.' He wouldn't train me to witness for Jesus Christ."

I asked, "What are you going to do about that?"

He said, "I need to find a new church." Now that is exactly the appropriate response if your pastor will not teach you to witness for Jesus Christ. Find another church. So we started to look to see if there was a church that would teach him, and the only church that I could find with a pastor who would train this 89-year-old man in EE was 21 miles away.

Can you imagine? Often the EE classes will end at 9 or 9:30 at night, and here was Robert, driving 21 miles down the highway in a Plymouth Fury to get home each week. Talk about prayer and faith. But you know what? He did it!

I did not see him again for another year. But when I saw him again, he was not hobbling on that cane quite so much; he was running down the aisle. He got up to the front and gave me the biggest hug, and I said to him, "Robert, I've been praying for you! Did you lead one person to Jesus?"

He said, "No, I've led five people to Jesus. Two of them were during the training but three of them were my friends. They were my neighbors. I always wanted to tell them about Jesus! I tried, but I didn't know how. Today, they are all Christians."

There was a hymn that we used to sing, that said, "Must I go and empty handed?"[67] In it, the idea that one would go to stand before his Lord and Savior, Jesus Christ with absolutely no one and nothing to show for all the years of service was anathema. Well, Robert did not want that to be said of him.

Robert was a good example of someone who many would have told to not bother with learning how to witness. And even though his pastor told him that he would not teach him, Robert did not listen to his pastor or the many; he listened to the One. The One who said, "You will be my witness."[68] Robert is a great example of a Christian who was not satisfied to stay where he was. He wanted the best day of his life to be his last day.

Now Robert isn't with us anymore; Robert is now in Heaven. But he did not go empty handed. He finished strong. What about you? Would you like your last days to

---

[67] Charles C. Luther, 1877. Luther heard Rev. A. G. Upham tell the story of a young man who was about to die. He'd only been a Christian for a month, and was sad because he'd had so little time to serve the Lord. He said, "I am not afraid to die; Jesus saves me now. But must I go empty handed?" This incident prompted the writing of the song; The complete song was first published in *Gospel Hymns No. 3*, 1878.

[68] Acts 1:8.

be your best? Would you like to finish strong? Let us consider what the Scriptures say in Hebrews 12:1-3:

> *Therefore we also, since we are surrounded by so great a cloud of witnesses, let us lay aside every weight, and the sin which so easily ensnares us, and let us run with endurance the race that is set before us, looking unto Jesus, the author and finisher of our faith, who for the joy that was set before Him endured the cross, despising the shame, and has sat down at the right hand of the throne of God. For consider Him who endured such hostility from sinners against Himself, lest you become weary and discouraged in your souls* (Hebrews 12:1-3).

These verses were written to the Hebrews to encourage them to persevere, to finish strong. They contain in them wisdom to help you and me to finish strong as well. You see finishing strong is not something that just happens. It is something that we as Christians should be working on. Let us look to these verses to learn how you and I, like Robert, can finish strong.

Notice as you start reading these verses the first word you run across. It is the word "therefore." Whenever you see the word "therefore," you have to ask yourself, what is it there for? In this case, it points us back to what has just occurred in Hebrews 11. The writer goes on to say, *"Since we are surrounded by so great that cloud of witnesses."* The intention here is to require us to look back at what has gone on before. So our first help in finishing strong is to consider history.

HISTORY

It helps me to consider the history around me. I sometimes study at an antique desk. The finish is cracked. The corners are rounded. The chair creaks. Some people would tell me to get a new desk that does not look so old and outdated, but other preachers have used this desk. Many very fine preachers. And studying at that desk causes me to consider those that have gone before me. In a way that is the image of this passage. We are to look back at those who have gone before us.

Some people read about this "cloud of witnesses," and imagine an Olympic runner coming into a stadium listening to the applause of the crowd all around him. If that, however, is how you see this passage, you are missing a big point. As we look back into Hebrews 11, this "cloud of witnesses" were people who were heavily persecuted for the cause of the gospel. They were beaten, stoned, and sawn in two for their Christianity. So a better image would be that of a runner sprinting into a stadium filled with people who had already won the gold medal. They are people who have finished the race strongly, and encourage you to do the same. You can hear them scream, "Keep going! Don't look back. You can do it!" Those in the "cloud of witnesses" have struggled and labored and sacrificed and in many cases gave their very lives to win the prize.

So, as you run this race, you must consider these heroes of the past who have run the race and won. You have got to see yourself in that kind of context like God does. We must consider history. And if we do, you can see how having that kind of vision would help you to finish strong.

HURDLES

A second help the writer to the Hebrews gives us is to encourage us to consider the hurdles we will encounter. Perhaps you have heard the saying, "It's not what people tell you that gets you into trouble, it's what they don't tell you." Even if you have not heard it you know the concept. So many times in life, others do not tell you the bad news until you are waist deep in the thing. Then they say, "Oh yea, I forgot to tell you..." Right. Thanks. Now it is too late. But here, the idea is exactly the opposite. The writer is telling you to consider the hard stuff right now. In fact, you will never finish strong unless you do.

The writer to the Hebrews points out two hurdles that will get in the way of you finishing strong. One is the stuff you hang on to. In verse 1 we are told to *"lay aside every weight."* If you are going to go far, you have got to go light. To run the race God has given us, we must put aside everything that hinders us. The clothing of a long-distance runner consists of shirt, shorts, and shoes that weigh less than a pound. On the track of faith, we are told to travel far. Therefore, we must travel light.

And yet, we hang on to "stuff" with all of our strength. We have got houses and cars and land and boats and condos and stocks. You name it. We have got it. Many times the image I get of some Christians is of a runner who would show up at the starting line with a huge backpack loaded down with all kinds of junk. Stuff piled way up on top and bungee corded to the side. Maybe he is towing a trailer with more junk. Do you think a person loaded down like that could ever finish a marathon? What would you say to someone you met like that? There is a great song by Steven Curtis Chapman that states, "I will hold on to the hand of my Savior, and I will hold on with all my might, I will hold loosely to things that are fleeting, and hold on to Jesus, I will hold on to Jesus for life."[69] Do not hang on to "stuff." 2 Peter makes it very clear what is going to happen to it. Put it aside and run.

The second hurdle the writer warns us about is sin, *"...let us put aside...the sin which so easily ensnares"* (vs. 1). Sin is a major impediment to the spiritual race. Sin is the enemy of persistence. Just in case we are a little confused about what we are being told to put aside, the Bible makes it painfully clear in many other places. Here are a few:

---

[69] Song by Steven Curtis Chapman recorded on his 1996 CD *Signs of Life*.

> *"But now you yourselves are to put off all these: anger, wrath, malice, blasphemy, filthy language out of your mouth. Do not lie to one another..."* (Colossians 3:8-9a).

> (Jesus talking) *"But take heed to yourselves, lest your hearts be weighed down with carousing, drunkenness, and cares of this life..."* (Luke 21:34).

Sin is a problem. You must deal with it. Put aside the stuff and the sin which so easily ensnares. It is easy to fall into, but you need to put sin aside to finish strong.

HEAT

Next, the writer to the Hebrews tells us that to truly finish strong we must consider the heat (not a temperature, but a round of a race or the heat of the battle that we have been called to). Your mission. Your "telos", or purpose.

Do you have a personal mission statement? It seems like everybody has a mission statement. "To boldly go where no one has gone before." Wow. Now that is a mission statement. What is your purpose?

Christians should have a goal. This is not an uncontrolled stroll through the byways of life. We are not tourists, we are pilgrims. Our race has been clearly marked out by God's Word. In 2 Timothy 4:7, Paul tells us that he has *"fought the good fight...finished the race...[and] kept the faith."* Was it just any old race that he felt like running or was it "the" race? Well, of course we know, it was "the" race.

How ridiculous it would be for a runner to show up at the New York Marathon and decide he did not like the course and start off in the wrong direction. Could he win the race? Of course not.

Now, I do not want you to get the wrong idea of this word "race." It is not talking about a gentle jog on a pretty spring day. This word "race" is the Greek word "agon" (ag-one, from which we get the word "agony"), which means conflict, fight, contention, battle. In Philippians it is translated "suffering," in Colossians it is translated "striving," in 1 Thessalonians it is "opposition," and in 1 and 2 Timothy it is "fight." It is a serious word about an intense struggle.

In 1 Corinthians 9, Paul goes into more detail about this race. He says:

> *Do you not know that those who run in a race all run, but one receives the prize? Run in such a way that you may obtain it. And everyone who competes for the prize is temperate in all things. Now they do it to obtain a perishable crown, but we for an imperishable crown. Therefore I run thus: not with uncertainty.* (If you go up a bit in the chapter you will see many of the things Paul does to run the race.) *Thus I fight: not as one who beats the air. But I discipline my body and bring it into subjection...* (verses 24-27).

Do you see the purpose here? Paul's goal was to complete the mission Christ had given him (and me—and you). Which was to win people to Jesus, build them in the faith, and send them to do the same. Nothing else mattered. He was willing to give his life in that pursuit.

During the Olympics, I was watching the gymnastic competition with my daughter Hannah, who was eight at the time. At one point she said, "I'm going to do that someday." I did not have the heart to point out that many of the girls in the Olympics had been in training for five to six years by the time they were her age. Most had given up all semblance of a normal life for this chance to compete in the games. And they did it for a chunk of metal.

What about you? Do you understand your calling? Have you gotten your marching orders? Have you gone into strict training? You need this mindset to finish strong.

HEAVENLY HOPE

Lastly, the writer gives us one other thing we need to do to finish strong. He tells us to "look to Jesus." To finish strong, we must consider our Heavenly Hope. We must consider Christ.

To look to Jesus you must look away from all others. Have you looked closely at this One you call your Savior? Do you see how seriously He took this race? We have the benefit of those that have gone before us. We have the benefit of our fellowship with our brothers and sisters.

Think about it. Alone Jesus stood at His trial. Alone He endured the agony of Gethsemane. Alone He endured the wrath of God at Calvary. Alone He took the greatest shame the men could think of. *"Cursed is everyone who hangs on a tree"* (Deuteronomy 21:23).

Jesus ran the race alone. You are not asked to do that. We are told, *"If you suffer [with Him], we shall reign with Him"* (2 Timothy 2:12 KJV). Jesus said, *"I'll never leave you nor forsake you"* (Hebrews 13:5). Jesus said, *"...lo, I am with you always, even to the end of the age"* (Matthew 28:20).

Considering Christ helps us to stand strong and finish strong. You see, no servant is greater than his Master. So, no matter how hard the race gets, consider Him.

Who has a family that does not understand your faith? Jesus came, and His own did not receive Him. Who has met with difficulty? Jesus met with willful unbelief and unmitigated opposition. Who has endured insults? Jesus was spat upon and called every name in the book. When you are challenged, look to Christ.

And on top of all of that, Jesus ran with joy. He knew what was coming. He could see the glory that was on the way.

Jesus pointed out in Luke 24:26: *"Ought not the Christ to have suffered these things and to enter into His glory?"*

An older lady was just about to die. While she was planning her funeral, the pastor came over to help her. They picked out all the hymns and decided what the service would look like and what verses she wanted him to read from the Bible. When everything was decided, the pastor prayed for her and got up to leave. She said, "One more thing, pastor. When you see me there in the casket, put a fork in my hand."

The pastor said, "Well, I'll do anything you ask, but I'm pretty sure someone's going to ask me why. So will you go ahead and tell me what I should say when they ask, 'Why does she have a fork in her hand?'"

She answered, "When I was a little girl, we'd have those potluck dinners on Sunday. Whenever they told you to keep your fork, it was because something good was on the way. We're not talking about pudding or something like that. We're talking cake or pie. Some reason we would want to keep our fork. You know what? I want everyone to know that I believe the good stuff is coming."

When we consider Christ, we see that He understood the glories that were coming. Peter says in 1 Peter 1:11: *"... searching what, or what manner of time, the Spirit of Christ who was in them was indicating when He testified beforehand the sufferings of Christ and the glories that would follow."*

The Christian life is so costly, but I'm telling you, dear reader, it is also so, so important. And you've been called to persevere. You've been called to run this race. You've been called to finish strong. And here is why: we all have a tendency to lose heart. Not all in one moment, but over time. Gradually slacking in resolve. And a corrective we are told in this passage is to look to the glorious object of our faith, and that is none other than Jesus, the Christ.

Consider Christ. When you understand what he endured for this cause, it will help you to finish strong. When you consider what He knows about the future, it will help you to finish strong. Run the race. It matters. Finish strong. It matters.

For many years, Dr. Kennedy would have called you, while he was on earth, a world-changer. It was one of the charter members of Coral Ridge that reminded Dr. Kennedy of something that he said back in the sixties to about 17 folks who were gathered on a Sunday evening service. After reading from Jeremiah 33:3 KJV, *"Call unto me, and I will answer thee and show thee great and mighty things which thou knowest not,"* he closed the Bible and said, "You know what? We can change the world!"

And look at what God has done. Everywhere I go in all of the world, I see the fruit of a congregation that was willing to believe. Even when it made no sense to believe that they could be part in changing the world.

Sometimes we get so caught up in daily living that we cannot see it. Steve Farrar, in his book *Finishing Strong*, told this story:

> If you could go back in a time machine, two thousand years ago, to the times of the New Testament, it might give you some perspective.

If you were to plant yourself in a busy market near the temple in Jerusalem, you could gather some real insight. Stop and think what it would be like to randomly interview the citizens of Jerusalem as they went about their daily business in the times of the early church.

You would only need to ask them a couple of questions.

"What do you think that people two thousand years from now will remember from your generation?"

My guess is, many of those citizens of the Roman Empire would answer, "Caesar Augustus." Others would respond, "Nero."

"But what about this group of people known as Christians. Don't you think that anyone will remember them or their leaders?"

"Are you kidding? That group of nobodies? They don't have any influence. They aren't important."

"You mean you haven't heard of Paul or Peter? Don't you think they'll be remembered? Or what about Mary or Martha? Wasn't their brother involved in some miracle?"

"I'm telling you, these people are insignificant. The only thing I ever hear of their leaders is that they are always winding up in jail. Trust me, in two thousand years, nobody will give them a thought."

So here we are, two thousand years later. And isn't it interesting that we name our children Peter and Paul, Mary and Martha? And we name our dogs Caesar and Nero.

You are doing something very significant, my friend. And He sees it. No wonder you're going to finish strong.[70]

CONCLUSION

We will finish strong not because we are so perseverant, but because He is so faithful; not because we are so strong, but because He is so mighty; not because we have run so well, but because He is the author and finisher of our faith. It is all because *"He who began a good work in you will complete it until the day of Jesus Christ"* (Philippians 1:6). When we cross that finish line, may we hear the words, *"Well done"* and give all the praise to Him Who has seen us through.

---

[70] Steve Farrar, *Finishing Strong* (Sister, OR, Multnomah Books, 1995), 219.

14

The Life Well-Lived

(Receive Your Eternal Reward)

In memory of D. James Kennedy, Ph.D.

"Well done, good and faithful servant; you were faithful over a few things, I will make you ruler over many things. Enter into the joy of your lord."

Matthew 25:21

Charles Dickens, in his *Tale of Two Cities* said, "It was the best of times, and it was the worst of times."[71] I think that now after Dr. Kennedy's passing, we can understand a bit of what he meant.

Since that Wednesday morning when Dr. Kennedy went home to be with Jesus, I've had a myriad of emotions, dipped together and intermingled.

On the one hand, we should feel a rush of excitement. Dr. Kennedy is enjoying Heaven at the feet of his Lord and Savior Jesus Christ! As Rev. Paul Hurst, one of the pastors at Coral Ridge Presbyterian Church, reminded the staff of

---

[71] Charles Dickens, *A Tale of Two Cities* (New York, NY: Signet Classic, 1997) 13.

Evangelism Explosion the week after his passing, Dr. Kennedy is totally healed. His back does not hurt, he has no trouble breathing, his mind is sharp, and his eyes are strong and fixed on the face of Jesus. He has seen Abraham and Isaac. Jacob and Noah. Paul, Peter, Thomas, and Timothy. Could there be anything more wonderful? So on one hand, we are filled with joy!

On the other hand, we are still here. And the road looks a little lonelier with the absence of D. James Kennedy leading the way.

I have had three great men in my life. My dad, who died when I was 23 and was a great man, a mentor, and my friend; Dr. Tom Stebbins, who led me to Jesus and taught me in the foundations of the faith; and Dr. D. James Kennedy, a great man of God who took the time to mentor me and guide me.

I received a great education at Knox Seminary. But I learned more from Dr. Kennedy by just being around him, asking questions, and watching him live out his life before Christ with excellence and passion.

There would be times when I would be struggling with classes. My head would be spinning with words and concepts, and I would ask Dr. Kennedy to explain it to me. He would say, "Well, it's simple. Here let me show you." He would draw out a diagram, and instantly I would understand. He was brilliant that way. He had this ability to take really hard stuff and bring it down to a level that anyone could understand.

One of the first questions that I ever asked Dr. Kennedy was, "How do I know if I'm a Calvinist?" Now, I have asked that question of many other pastors and professors just for fun, to see what they would say. I have been lectured to. I have been given long essays. I was even given a copy of Loraine Boettner's *Reformed Doctrine of Predestination*, which is a seriously serious book, and I highly recommend it. But what was Dr. Kennedy's answer? Now don't forget that he wrote *Truths that Transform*, which is a strong explanation of the reformed faith. He could have given me a copy. But what did he do?

He put his hand on my shoulder and asked, "John, have you ever prayed asking God to save someone you know? A friend, a relative, maybe someone you work with?" I said, "Sure, all the time." He said, "You know what John? You're a Calvinist. Don't worry about it. The rest will come."

I have enjoyed ten of the best years with Dr. Kennedy teaching me the doctrines of the faith. And for that I am eternally grateful. I am sure many reading this book could say the same thing and more about him.

Not only was he an awesome teacher, but also he was so passionate in how he lived out his life. I loved going to lunch with him. I would watch him. I would be waiting on the edge of his seat for God to show him who he was supposed to talk to. And he would ask two great questions, listen, and then share the greatest news those people ever heard about life through Jesus, and Him alone. And regardless of what anyone says, he still slapped his knee as he started into the Gospel. Sometimes we would fight over who would get to share.

One time I visited him in the hospital. When I walked in the room he caught my eye and nodded his head toward the nurse. I looked at him, puzzled, so he did it again. This time she saw him and said, "What? Now he's going to tell me about Jesus too?" Dr. Kennedy exclaimed, "Just let him share his testimony with you!"

I have had opportunities to go out on EE calls with him, and he was awesome. He was the real deal.

I miss him everyday.

So here we are, standing on this road that he (following Christ, of course) helped lead many to, and wondering, "What's next? Where do we go from here?"

Do you believe that the best days are yet to come? Many will say "yes," some "no." Some might say "yes" just because they think it is the right answer. What about you? Do you believe that the best is yet to come?

Dr. Kennedy believed that the best is yet to come! He believed in spiritual multiplication. This idea that as one trained another to train another that the Gospel would explode around the world. He often told me that when he got to Heaven he was going to get a lawn chair and sit by the front gate and watch as the results of spiritual multiplication poured in. He could not wait the see the fruit.

I have gone on round-the-world trips and have seen some of the fruit that Dr. Kennedy was hoping for. In 2009 alone, by the grace of God, we were able to train 238,000 people in the ministry of Evangelism Explosion. In the process, we saw over 5.2 million people make a profession of faith in Jesus Christ.

My life is dedicated to continuing, as God makes me able, this spiritual multiplication. And through it, I believe with all my heart, that the best is yet to come.

I was talking with Anne Kennedy, and she reminded me that to believe such things is a matter of faith. It is a matter of what you are trusting in. And she is right. It is a matter, purely and simply, of faith. But not everyone believes.

I listened to a popular Christian radio show a while back where the announcer and guest both agreed that you cannot ask people about eternal life in an eastern culture without causing offense. I read an article that same month from a famous preacher who said the topic of eternal life was off limits in the west as well. So with all this negative talk about the effectiveness of personal evangelism it is easy to think twice about witnessing to someone that you meet, or even a close friend.

I guess the question at its heart is what you believe about what God said regarding the effectiveness of the proclamation of the Gospel and the preparation of the hearts of men and women to receive it. Either the fields are ripe unto harvest or they are not. What do you believe?

That day that I heard the radio show, Archbishop Harry Goodhew (a member of EE's International Board of Directors) and I were walking near the harbor in Hong Kong. While we walked and talked, a college-age Chinese girl approached us and began to ask us questions. Soon we could see that she wanted to talk to us about Jesus. She was out with her youth group, and they were seeing if there were some folks who wanted to know how to get to Heaven. When she heard that we were Christians, she beamed. When we asked her why God would let her into Heaven, she said, "I believe in Jesus! He died for me!"

This girl must not have heard the radio show saying that you could not talk about Heaven within the eastern world. Or if she did, she refused to believe it.

Witnessing (which is a big part of the idea that the best is yet to come) is, after all, a decision about what you believe. It is first and primarily a matter of faith.

So as we are looking at the road before us, I think we need to talk about faith.

FULL OF FAITH

We were gathered together in the choir room on a Thursday night. This was one of the upper levels of Evangelism Explosion training. This particular night the teacher was Dr. D. James Kennedy. His topic was faith.

He caught the attention of a young man on the front row and said, "Young man, don't move! Not even a muscle! You have a poisonous snake under you chair. Don't look! He's looking right at your leg. When he looks away I'll tell you. Be ready to jump out of that chair. Steady. Wait. JUMP!" That young man nearly jumped through the roof! I think we all jumped!

The point that Dr. Kennedy was making was simple. If that young man really believed him, had faith in what he said—that there was a poisonous snake under the chair—that young man's belief would have certainly, logically, radically turned to action. True belief, or true faith, always leads to action.

And it must. Because faith, according to the writer to the Hebrews, is the substance of things hoped for, the evidence of things not seen.

Faith is the substance, the assurance, of things hoped for. It is the evidence, the proof, the conviction of the reality of things not seen. Faith perceives as real fact what is not revealed to the senses.

Part of the confusion comes from the fact that we use faith everyday. Every time we flip a light switch, it is an exercise in faith. We really believe our action will lead to a result—in this case the illumination of a light. Or every time we insert our car keys into our car's ignition, we expect that it will start. But the challenge is that these things are temporal and prone to failure. Sometimes light bulbs burn out and for some of us, the action of trying to start our cars is more of an act of futility than an act of faith.

But spiritual faith, true saving faith, is not just a hope, a dream, or even simply a promise of something that may or may not be.

Faith is the substance. The reality. It is holding the title to the thing hoped for. If you hold the title to a piece of land you have never seen, your lack of seeing the land has no bearing on its ownership. Holding the title is surety of your ownership.

The world says, "Seeing is believing." But in Hebrews 11 we are told that "Believing is seeing." But not because of faith itself or even the amount of faith that we have but because of the object of our faith—God. Verse 6 says, *"...for he who comes to God must believe that He is, and He is a rewarder of those who diligently seek Him."*

In the close of the previous chapter, the writer to the Hebrews spoke of faith as a principle of the spiritual life. He quoted a famous phrase from Habakkuk 2:4, *"...the just shall live by faith."*[72] And now the writer proceeds to vindicate its truth in a series of brilliant biographical illustrations. Illustrations that I hope give us encouragement and, in some cases, cause us pause.

---

[72] Actually, this is a quote from Romans 1:17, which is quoting Habakkuk 2:4 which reads: *"The just shall live by his faith."*

The first time I remember really studying this passage was in the fall of 1996. My wife Ann and I believed that God had called us to the ministry. That Sunday morning I had told my pastor that we were going on staff with Evangelism Explosion. He called us crazy sixty times in sixty seconds. He said, "You're crazy, crazy, crazy, crazy, crazy, crazy, crazy, crazy, crazy, crazy, crazy!"

He had heard of EE's financial woes and generally believed that EE could not pay us.

I have to tell you, when your pastor calls you crazy sixty times in sixty seconds, it is a bit discouraging. So that afternoon I called down to speak with Tom Stebbins, but Tom was not home—he was out preaching somewhere—so I talked to his wife, Donna. Donna said, "Listen, I'm not even going to talk to you until you have read Hebrews 11." Hebrews 11, of course, is the hall of fame of faith. As Ann and I read the chapter, illustrations of people's lives flooded over us.

There is the story of Abraham. He left his home because God told him to. He did not know where he was going but God said, "Trust me. I've got it covered." And God told him, "Your seed is going to be like the stars and the whole world will be blessed through you." Through a grand miracle God gives him a son, and then God tells Abraham to kill his son—the one through whom the promise was made. This chapter tells us a bit of that day when Abraham got up and took that boy whom he loved and headed out of the house.

It had to have been hard on Abraham to even consider killing this beloved son, but he acted because he believed that God would keep his promise. He planned to kill the boy and was counting on the fact that God would raise the boy from the dead just to keep his promise. That was his plan.

Think about it. There was nothing that his eyes had ever seen that would have suggested that this could happen. Had he tried to explain his plan to anyone they would have called him, "Crazy." But Abraham believed God.

Another person mentioned here is Rahab who kept the spies when they were scouting out Jericho. She knew that anyone who helped spies would be killed. Now she could have either believed what she saw was true, or she could believe what the men of God said was true, that she'd be protected. She chose to trust God and not man.

In this chapter we are told that this faith was why God was not ashamed to be called their God.

As we read these accounts, a peace flowed over Ann and I and enveloped us. We were only too happy to be called crazy for the sake of faith. I once heard Chuck Swindoll say, "Nothing that is under God's control is ever out of control." It is about God and what we believe about Him.

Their faith was made evident through the actions that flowed from their faith, as Dr. Kennedy taught us. The whole book of James is illustrative about the role of works in the substance of faith. The point—true faith acts while psuedo-faith, or fake faith, does not.

Now, in the Parable of the Talents, two servants act on their faith and are called faithful. *"Well done, good and faithful servant."* We have been looking at this passage pretty much this entire book, but still have not asked a very important question: What does it mean to be faithful?

When someone steps out in faith, and does what God commands them, we call that person "faithful." Full of faith. When you or I become full of faith, we faithfully do what it is that God has given us to do. We act on the well of faith within us. Abraham and Rahab are just a few examples of faithful people. What about you? Are you full of faith? Are you so full that your cup is overflowing into actions?

THE FAITHFUL FOLLOWER

The reason why this last chapter is called "The Life Well-Lived" is because I can think of no greater example of a life of faith than that of D. James Kennedy. He was faithful in most everything he did. He believed in excellence in all things, and all things to God's glory. I hope that can be an encouragement to both you and me as we look at this road that God has called us to.

In faith, Jim Kennedy quit his lucrative position as a dance teacher and walked out the door with nothing but thirteen dollars to his name. He felt the call of God to quit the job, even though he had no idea what to do then.

In faith, he took a small pastorate in Fort Lauderdale, Florida because God closed the door on his ability to go to Africa as a missionary. He had no idea that in that small church God would open his eyes to see the fields ripe for harvest. Evangelism Explosion was created for the purpose of reaching that harvest for God. He also hadn't a clue that the small church of seventeen people, Coral Ridge Presbyterian Church, would sky rocket to the fastest growing Presbyterian Church in America for fifteen years.

In faith, he started Knox Seminary and Westminster Academy to educate Christian families, future pastors, and budding theologians in the truth of the Bible, encouraging them to go forth sharing the gospel and changing the world.

In faith, Dr. Kennedy founded Coral Ridge Ministries and WAFG 90.3 to reach local, national, and international audiences with truth about who Jesus is, the truth of the Bible, and the love of Christ—the One who loved them enough to die for them.

In faith, he continued EE at Coral Ridge Presbyterian Church until there was so many pastors writing him asking what he was doing to make the church grow that he started inviting them and taking them out witnessing—exactly what Kennedy Smart did for him. EE grew and grew until it formed an International Board of Directors and went global. Today, EE is in every country on the earth sharing with people groups of every shape and size telling them the most important news that they will ever hear. It was unacceptable to Dr. Kennedy for there to be a person on this earth who had never heard the name of Jesus, so he persevered in faith unto the end of his life, preaching and sharing the Good News to the ends of the earth.

Most of the time Jim Kennedy had no idea where he would get the funds for all of the ministries, but God always provided. And through faith, he continued doing everything he possibly could to reach people, love people, and share with people how they could spend eternity in Heaven with God.

Anyone might think that with a church, many ministries, countless books, broadcasts to be done, and a radio program that Dr. Kennedy's greatest faithfulness lied in running it all. Even though that must have taken a great deal of patience, perseverance, leadership, and faithfulness, there is a better, more humble picture that truly shows how faith-filled he was.

Dr. Jerry Newcombe, co-writer of many books with Dr. Kennedy, said, "On a given Thursday night, where was Dr. Kennedy? He was at the EE program in a little hall teaching laypeople from the church how to witness. Throughout forty-seven years of ministry at Coral Ridge Presbyterian Church, it never changed. That speaks volumes. He had books that were read all over the world, founded Evangelism Explosion which reaches to every part of the globe...I mean, the impact was amazing, and yet every Thursday night, where would you find Dr. Kennedy? You would find him out on On-The-Job Training, sharing with a waitress or a homeless man or a woman doing laundry."

Rich Devos, one of Dr. Kennedy's dearest friends, said, "Jim Kennedy has one goal in life, and that is to present the Gospel and win people to Jesus. That's his whole focus in life. His dream is to reach the world. And I'm sure, now that he's in Heaven, he can count all the souls that are in Heaven because of him all over the world that he either witnessed to or that indirectly were witnessed to because of his leadership and the things he encouraged and trained people to do."[73]

Dr. Kennedy really was the real deal. He was a man of high integrity—humble in words and actions. He was quick to give credit to others and always thrilled to hear about people coming to know Jesus as Lord and Savior. To me, he was a personal friend, a mentor, and a model of how to keep equipping the saints for ministry. He never wavered from that priority; and because of that, he challenged hundreds of thousands of people across the world to be witnesses for Christ. I know I will certainly miss Jim Kennedy.

---

[73] *A Lamplighter For Christ* (Fort Lauderdale, FL: Coral Ridge Ministries, 2007) 24.

He was a leader—not on just the organizational chart of ministries, but on the frontlines. He could truly say, as Jesus said, "Follow me." This may sound like hyperbole to you, but I don't consider it so. God used Moses to deliver more than a million people from captivity and slavery. Well, God used D. James Kennedy to deliver hundreds of millions from the captivity and slavery of sin.

Why God chooses to use individuals like Dr. Kennedy for such grand purposes is, quite frankly, a mystery. But He does, and His work is marvelous in our eyes. I praise God for the life of Dr. D. James Kennedy. As a result of his faithful labor, all over the world, this Gospel is bearing fruit and growing.

CONCLUSION

But now, we must ask the question, what about us? I hope this book has encouraged you to keep on walking the road we Christians are called to be on. I also hope you are encouraged to, like Dr. Kennedy, live a faith-filled life. Even though he is no longer on that road with us, we know One who is. One who will never leave our side, watching our faith turn into action before His eyes. And one day, when all is said and done, we can go to eternal rest with Him. He will be with us in the hard times, He promises; and at the end of the road, He will carry us home. There, in the warmth and safety of His arms, He will say, "Well done, My good and faithful servant. Well done."

Dear reader, the best is yet to come. Do you believe that? I certainly do. Fight the fight. Run the race. Be a light. Live for others. Be a faith-filled doer. Serve your Master. And all the glory goes to the One who deserves it all, our Beloved Shepherd.

Afterword

Preparing for the Only Day in Your
Life that Really Matters

by D. James Kennedy, Ph.D

There is really only one day in the life of anybody that counts. Pardon me? Not the day of birth? Not the day of baptism? Not the day of entering school? Not the day of confirmation (depending on your tradition)? Not the day of graduation? Not the day of marriage? Not the day of landing a great job? Not the day of the birth of a child? Not the day of retirement? Not the day of death? All of these are important, of course, but the only day in your life that really counts is the day when you stand before Jesus Christ, after death. Either He will look you in the eye and say, *"Well done, you good and faithful servant"* or He will say, *"Depart from me, you cursed, for I never knew you."* In between these two extremes, it is fair to say that He may say to some: "Well, you can come in, but I am really disappointed in how poorly you finished."

Paul tells us that some will be saved, but as through fire. On the Day of Judgment, their works will not stand the test of Christ. They themselves will be saved, but their works will be shown to be wood, hay, and stubble.[74]

The purpose of this book is to prepare you for the only day in your life that really counts. Our goal is that you will put into practice those things Jesus has taught us in His Word, so that He will say to us: *"Well done, My good and faithful servant."*

---

[74] 1 Corinthians 3:12.

Index

Z